# The Unseen Hand and Other Plays

Forensic & the Navigators
The Holy Ghostly
Back Bog Beast Bait
Shaved Splits
4-H Club

## Other Plays by Sam Shepard

# The Unseen Hand
# and Other Plays
## by Sam Shepard

APPLAUSE
THEATRE BOOK PUBLISHERS
100 West 67 St. • New York, N.Y. 10023 • (212) 496-7511
ISBN 0-87910-203-9                    $ 9.95

Library of Congress Cataloging in Publication Data

Shepard, Sam, 1943–
    The unseen hand and other plays.

    Reprint of the 1972 ed. published by Bobbs-Merrill,
Indianapolis.
    CONTENTS: The unseen hand.--Forensic & the navigators.
--The holy ghostly.--Back bog beast bait.--(etc.)
    I. Title.
PS3569.H394U5    1981    812'.54    80-27628

ISBN 0-89396-040-3 (cloth)
       0-89396-041-1 (paper)

# Contents

*"This is dedicated to the one I love"*—
**O-Lan**

# The Unseen Hand

THE UNSEEN HAND was first produced at the La Mama Experimental Theatre Club on Friday, December 26, 1969 with the following cast:

Blue Morphan ........................Beeson Carrol
Willie (The Space Freak) ................Lee Kissman
Cisco Morphan ....................Bernie Warkenton
The Kid .............................Sticks Carlton
Sycamore Morphan .................Victor Eschbach

This production was directed by Jeff Bleckner; settings by Fred Katz; lighting by Johnny Dodd; sound by Charles Mingus III; music by Beeson Carroll; stage manager, Burton Greenhouse.

It was subsequently presented by Albert Poland at the Astor Place Theatre on April 1, 1970 with the following cast:

Blue Morphan ........................Beeson Carrol
Willie (The Space Freak) ................Lee Kissman
Cisco Morphan ........................David Selby
The Kid ............................David Clennon
Sycamore Morphan .....................Tom Rosica

This production was directed by Jeff Bleckner; settings by Santo Loquasto; costumes by Linda Fisher; lighting by Roger Morgan; music by Paul Conly, featuring Lothar and the Hand People.

## Scene:

Center stage is an old '51 Chevrolet convertible, badly bashed and dented, no tires and the top torn to shreds. On the side of it is written "Kill Azusa" with red spray paint. All around is garbage, tin cans, cardboard boxes, Coca-Cola bottles and other junk. The stage is dark. Sound of a big diesel truck from a distance, then getting louder, then passing with a whoosh. As the sound passes across the stage the beam of the headlights cuts through the dark and passes across the Chevy. Silence. Soft blue moonlight comes up slowly as the sound of another truck repeats, as before, its headlights cutting through the dark. This should be a synchronized tape-light loop which repeats over and over throughout the play—the headlights sweeping past accompanied by the sound of a truck. The lights come up but maintain a full moon kind of light. The whooshing of the trucks and the passing lights keep up. A figure slowly emerges out of the back seat of the Chevy. His name is BLUE MORPHAN. He has a scraggly beard, black overcoat, blue jeans, cowboy boots and hat and a bottle in his hand.

> *He is slightly drunk and talks to an imaginary driver in the front seat.*

**Blue**

Say listen. Did we pass Cucamunga? Didn't we already pass it up? Listen. This here is Azuza. We must a' passed it up. Why don't ya pull up on the embankment there and let me out? Come on now. Fair's fair. I didn't stab ya' or nothin'. Nobody stole yer wallet, did they? OK. So let me out like I ask ya'. That's it. Atta' boy. OK. Good. If I had me any loose jingle I'd sure lay it on ya' fer gas money but I'd like to get me a cup a'coffee. You know how it is. Thanks, boy.

> *He slowly climbs out of the back seat onto the stage, then reaches into the back and pulls out a battered guitar with broken strings.*

If ya' ever happen through Duarte let me know. Gimme a buzz or something. Drop me a line. 'Course ya' don't got the address but that's all right. Just ask 'em fer Blue Morphan. That's me. Anyone. Just ask any old body fer old Blue. They'll tell ya'.

> *He pulls out an old dusty suitcase held together with rope and sets it on the ground, then a rifle.*

I ain't been back there fer quite a spell now but they'll be able to direct ya' to the stables all right. Follow the old Union Pacific till ya' come to Fish Creek. Don't pick up no longhairs though. Now I warned ya'. OK. OK. Do what ya' like but I warned ya'.

> *He pulls out a broken bicycle, a fishing rod, a lantern, an inner tube, some pipe, a bag full of bolts and other junk. He keeps taking more and more stuff out of the back seat and setting it down on the stage as he talks.*

You been driving long enough by now to tell who to pick up and who to leave lay. But if they got their thumb out you better look 'em over twice. I know. I used to drive a Chevy myself. Good car. Thing is nowadays it ain't so easy to tell the riff-raff from the gentry. Know what I mean. You can get tricked. They can fool ya'. All kinda fancy over-the-head talk and all along they're workin' for the government same as you. I mean you might not be. Like me fer instance. I'm a free agent. Used to be a time when I'd take an agency job. Go out and bring in a few bush-wackers just for the dinero. Usually a little bonus throwed in. But nowadays ya' gotta keep to yerself. They got nerve gas right now that can kill a man in 30 seconds. Yup. A drop a' that on the back of a man's hand and poof! Thirty seconds. That ain't all. They got rabbit fever, parrot fever and other stuff stored up. Used to be, a man would have hisself a misunderstanding and go out and settle it with a six gun. Now it's all silent, secret. Everything moves like a fever. Don't know when they'll cut ya' down and when they do ya' don't know who done it. Don't mean to get ya' riled though. Too nice a night fer that. Straight, clean highway all the way from here to Tuba City. Shouldn't have no trouble. If yer hungry though there's a Bob's Big Boy right up the road a piece. I don't know if ya' go in fer double decker cheeseburgers or not but—Listen, tell ya' what, long as yer hungry I'll jest come along with ya' a ways and we'll chow down together. Sure. Good idea. I ain't ate since yesterday mornin' anyhow. Just before ya' picked me up.

*He starts putting all the junk back into the car.*

Sure is nice of ya' to help me out this a way. Don't come across many good old boys these days. Seems like they all got a chip on the shoulder or somethin'. You noticed that? The way they swagger around givin' ya' that look. Like ya' weren't no more than a road apple or somethin' worse. If they'd a known me in my prime it might change their tune. Hadn't a been fer the old hooch here I'd a been in history books by now. Probably am anyhow, under a different name. They never get the name straight. Don't matter too much anyhow. Least it don't hurt my feelings none. 'Course yer too young to remember the Morphan brothers probably. Cisco, Sycamore and me, Blue. The three of us. 'Course we had us a few more. Not a gang exactly. Not like these teen-age hot rodders with their

Mercurys and Hudson Hornets. Least ways we wasn't no menace. The people loved us. The real people I'm talkin' about. The people people. They helped us out in fact. And vica versa. We'd never go rampant on nobody. Say, you oughta' get yer tires checked before ya' go too much further. That left rear one looks a little spongey. Can't be too careful when yer goin' a distance. A car's like a good horse. You take care a' it and it takes care a' you.

> WILLIE, *the space freak, enters. He is young and dressed in super future clothes, badly worn and torn. Orange tights, pointed shoes, a vinyl vest with a black shirt that comes up like a hood over the back of his head. His skin is badly burned and blistered with red open sores. His head is shaved and there is a black hand print burned into the top of his skull. At moments he goes into convulsive fits, his whole body shaking. He staggers on stage. BLUE sees him and stops his babble. They stare at each other for a moment.*

I suppose yer lookin' fer a handout or somethin'.

> WILLIE *just stares. Exhausted, his sides heaving,* BLUE *climbs back into the back seat and disappears. His voice can still be heard.*

That's the trouble with you kids. Always lookin' fer a handout. There ain't nothin' romantic about panhandlin', sonny. Ye' ain't gonna' run across the holy grail thataway. Anyhow ya' come to the wrong place. This here is Azusa, not New York City.

> BLUE's *head pops up from the back seat. He looks at* WILLIE *still standing there, panting.*

"A," "Z," "U," "S," "A." "Everything from 'A' to 'Z' in the USA." Azusa. If yer thinking on robbin' me a' my worldly possessions you can take a look for yerself. I been livin' in this Chevy for twenty years now and I ain't come across no diamond rings yet.

> *He disappears back down in the back seat.*

'Course if ya' just wanna' rest that's a different story. It's a free highway. Yer welcome to stay a spell. The driver's seat's mighty comfortable once ya' get used to the springs.

**Willie**
You Blue Morphan?
> *A pause as* BLUE *slowly rises, his head coming into view.*

**Blue**
What'd you call me?

**Willie**
Is your name Blue Morphan?

**Blue**
Look, sonny, nobody knows my name or where I been or where I'm goin'. Now you better trot along.
> *He sinks back down.*

**Willie**
I've traveled through two galaxies to see you. At least you could hear me out.
> BLUE's *head comes back into view.*

**Blue**
You been hittin' the juice or somethin'? What's yer name, boy?

**Willie**
They call me Willie.

**Blue**
Who's they?

**Willie**
The High Commission.

**Blue**
What're ya' shakin' for? It's a warm night. Here. Have a swig a' this. It'll put a tingle in ya'.
> *He offers* WILLIE *the bottle.*

**Willie**
No thanks.

**Blue**
What, Apple Jack ain't good enough for ya', huh? Suppose you run in fancy circles or somethin'. Just a second, just a second.
> *He climbs out of the back seat and goes around to the trunk and opens it. He starts rummaging through junk in the trunk as* WILLIE *stands there shaking.*

Got a couple a Navajo blankets here in the back some-

wheres. Keep 'em special fer when the wind comes up.
Sometimes it blows in off the San Joaquin and gets a bit
nippy. Ah, here ya' go. This oughta' do it.

> *He pulls out a dusty Indian blanket from the trunk and takes
> it over to* WILLIE.

Here ya' go. Here. Well, take it.

> *He offers the blanket to* WILLIE, *but* WILLIE *just stares at
> him, shaking and trembling.*

You sure got yerself a case a the DT's there, boy. Here.
Wrap this around ya'. Come on now.

> BLUE *wraps the blanket around* WILLIE's *shoulders, then
> notices the handprint on his head.*

What's that ya' got on yer head there? Some new fashion
or somethin'?

**Willie**

The brand.

**Blue**

Like they do with steers, ya' mean? Who done it to ya'?

**Willie**

The Sorcerers of the High Commission. It's why I've come.

**Blue**

You better come over here and sit down. I can't make hide
nor hair out a what yer sayin'. Come on. Have a seat and
collect yerself.

> *He leads* WILLE *over to the car, opens the front door and
> seats him in the driver's seat. Blue climbs up on the front
> fender and sits.*

Now what's this here High Commission stuff? Why would
they wanna put a brand on yer head?

**Willie**

I can't see where I'm driving if you're going to sit there.

**Blue**

Say, what's yer game, boy? Any fool can see this Chevy
ain't got no wheels.

**Willie**

We used to shoot deer and strap them over the hood.

**Blue**

Forget the deer. What's this brand business?

**Willie**
I've been zeroed.
**Blue**
What's that mean?
**Willie**
Whenever I think beyond a certain circumference of a certain circle there's a hand that squeezes my brain.
**Blue**
What hand?
**Willie**
It's been burned in. You can't see it now. All you can see is the scar.
**Blue**
And this High Commission fella did this to ya'?
**Willie**
It's not a fella. It's a body. Nobody ever sees it. Just the sorcerers.
**Blue**
Who's that?
**Willie**
Black magicians who know the secrets of the Nogo.
**Blue**
I'll have to make a left turn on that one, sonny. I'm a simple man. I eat simple. I talk simple and I think simple.
**Willie**
That's why we need you.
**Blue**
We?
**Willie**
The prisoners of the Diamond Cult.
**Blue**
Just talk. I'll listen.
**Willie**
I am descended from a race of mandrills. Fierce baboons that were forced into human form by the magic of the Nogo. It was decided since we were so agile and efficient at sorting out diamonds for the Silent Ones that we could

be taken a step further into human form and tested as though we were still baboons but give results in the tests as though we were human.

**Blue**

What kinda' tests?

**Willie**

Mind warps. Time splits. Electro-laser fields. Dimensional overlays. Spatial projections. Force fields.

**Blue**

But you think like a man?

**Willie**

And feel. This was a mistake the sorcerers had not counted on. They wanted an animal to develop that was slightly sub-human, thereby to maintain full control over its psychosomatic functions. The results were something of the opposite. We developed as super-human entities with capacities for thought and feeling far beyond that of our captors. In order to continue their tests they needed an invention to curtail our natural reasoning processes. They came up with the Unseen Hand, a muscle contracting syndrome hooked up to the will of the Silent Ones. Whenever our thoughts transcend those of the magicians the Hand squeezes down and forces our minds to contract into non-preoccupation.

**Blue**

What's that like?

**Willie**

Living death. Sometimes when one of us tries to fight the Hand or escape its control, like me, we are punished by excruciating muscle spasms and nightmare visions. Blood pours past my eyes and smoke fills up my brain.

**Blue**

What do ya' want me to do about all this? I'm just a juicer on the way out.

**Willie**

You're more than that. The sorcerers and the Silent Ones of the High Commission have lost all touch with human emotion. They exist in almost a purely telepathic intellectual state. That is why they can still exert control over our race. You and your brothers are part of another world, far beyond anything the High Commission has experienced. If you came into Nogoland blazing your six guns they wouldn't have any idea how to deal with you. All their technology and magic would be at a total loss. You would be too real for their experience.

**Blue**
Now hold on there, whatever yer name was.

**Willie**
Willie.

**Blue**
Yeah. Well, first off, my brothers are dead. Cisco and Sycamore was gunned down in 1886.

**Willie**
It doesn't matter.

**Blue**
Well, unless yer counting on bringin' 'em back from the grave it matters a whole lot.

**Willie**
That's exactly what I'm counting on.

> BLUE *jumps down from the fender and grabs the rifle. He points it at* WILLIE.

**Blue**
All right, wiseacre. Out a' the car. Come on or I'll plug ya' right here on the spot.

**Willie**
You can't plug me, Blue. I don't die.

**Blue**
Not ever?

**Willie**
Never.

**Blue**
Then how come yer so scared to take on them High Commandos yer own self?

**Willie**
Because of the Hand.

> WILLIE *goes into a violent spasm, clutching his head in*

*agony.* BLUE *drops the rifle and goes to* WILLIE. *He pulls him out of the car and sets him on the ground.*

**Blue**

Now stop jumpin' around, yer makin' me nervous. Just settle down. You want the cops to catch us?

*WILLIE writhes on the ground and screams phrases and words as though warding off some unseen terror.*

**Willie**

Wind refraction! Cyclone riff! Get off the rim! Off the rim!

**Blue**

What's with you, boy?

**Willie**

The latitudinal's got us! Now! Now! Smoke it up! Smoke him! Gyration forty zero two nodes! Two nodes! You got the wrong mode! Wrong! Correction! Correct that! Step! Stop it! Modulate eighty y's west! Keep it west! Don't let up the field rays! Keep it steady on! Harmonic rhythm scheme! Harmony four! Discord! You got it! Aaah! Aaaaaaaah! Let up! Extract! Implode! Bombard the picture! The picture! Image contact! Major! Minor! Loop syndrome! Drone up! Full drone wave! Now! Oooooh! Just about! Just about! Crystallize fragment mirror! Keep it keen! Sharpen that focus! Hypo filament! Didactachrome! Resolve! Resolve! Resolve! Reverb! Fuzz tone! Don't let the feedback in! Feed it back! Keep your back up! Back it up! Reverse foilage meter! Fauna scope. Graphic tableau. Gramophonic display key. All right. All right. Now raise the horizon. Good. Moon. Planets in place. Heliographic perspective. Atmosphere checking cool. Galactic four count. Star meter gazing central focus. Beam to head on sunset. Systol reading ace in. Dystol balance. Treble boost. All systems baffled. Baffled.

*WILLIE goes unconscious.* CISCO MORPHAN *enters. He wears a serape, jeans, cowboy hat and boots, a bandana on his head, a rifle and a hand gun. He has long black hair and scraggly beard. He is younger than* BLUE *by about twenty years.*

**Cisco**
Blue!
> *He goes to* BLUE *with his arms out.*

Well, don't ya' recognize me, boy? It's me! Cisco. Yer
brother. Yer mean ornery old flesh and blood.

**Blue**
Just stand back, mister. I'm gettin' rid a' this right now.
> *He throws his bottle behind the car and holds his rifle on*
> CISCO.

**Cisco**
Still foxey as ever, ain't ya'. Better watch out that thing
don't go off by accident. Let a gun go to rustin' like that
and ya' never can tell what it's liable to do.

**Blue**
It's plenty greased enough to open daylight in the likes
of an imposter.

**Cisco**
Oh. So ya' don't believe it's really me, huh. Let's see.
What if I was to show ya' some honest to God proof of
the puddin'?

**Blue**
Like what, fer instance?

**Cisco**
Like say a knife scar ya' give me fer my sixteenth birth-
day in Tuscaloosa.

**Blue**
That'd do just fine.

**Cisco**
All right. Now you hold yer fire there while I get out a'
my poncho.

**Blue**
Just hurry it up.
> CISCO *sets down his rifle and starts taking off his serape as*
> BLUE *holds the rifle on him.*

**Cisco**
Yeah, I guess yer plenty busy nowadays.

**Blue**

How da ya' mean? Keep yer hand away from that pistol.

**Cisco**

There we go. Now. Take a looksee.

> CISCO.*takes off his poncho and shows* BLUE *a long scar going from the middle of his back all the way around to his chest.* BLUE *examines it closely.*

What ya' got to say now? Ain't that the mark ya' give me with yer very own fishing knife?

**Blue**

Sure beats the hell outa' me.

**Cisco**

If yer satisfied why don't ya' do me a favor and lower that buffalo gun.

> BLUE *lowers his rifle as* CISCO *puts his poncho back on.*

**Blue**

But you and Sycamore was gunned down in the street right in broad daylight. I was there.

**Cisco**

You escaped. Sycamore should be comin' up any second now.

**Blue**

I don't get it, Cisco. What's goin' on?

**Cisco**

Seems there's certain unfinished business. This must be the fella here.

**Blue**

You know this looney?

**Cisco**

Let's take a look. He ain't dead, is he?

> CISCO *leans over* WILLIE *and looks at his face.*

**Blue**

Damned if I can tell. He just shows up out a' the clear blue and starts to jawin' about outer space and High Commancheros and what all. I can't make it out.

**Cisco**

He came alone?

**Blue**

So far. First him and then you. You know somethin' I don't, Cisco?

**Cisco**

All I know is that I was summoned up. Me, you and Sycamore is gonna be back in action before too long. And this here dude is gonna set us straight on what the score is.

**Blue**

What score? I settled up all my debts a long time ago. I hunted down every last one a' them varmints what got you and Sycamore. I'm an old man, Cisco.

**Cisco**

There's other upstarts seems to be jammin' up the works. Besides, I'll be glad to see a little action for a change. I been hibernatin' for too long now. You got any grub layin' around here somewhere?

**Blue**

Best I can do is Campbell's Pork and Beans, Cisco. Have to be cold out a' the can too. Can't make no fires on account a' the Highway Patrol.

**Cisco**

What's that?

**Blue**

The law. Like the old Texas Rangers, 'cept they got cars now.

> BLUE *goes to the car and opens the trunk. He rummages around for a can of beans.*

**Cisco**

Well, looks like you got yerself a nice enough campsite. What's this here rig?

**Blue**

Fifty-one Chevy. Don't make 'em like this any more. Now they got dual headlights, twin exhausts, bucket seats, wrap around windshields and what all. Extra junk to make it look fancy. Don't go no better though.

> CISCO *sits in the driver's seat and turns the steering wheel.*

Must take a hefty team to pull this load. What's it made out of, iron or somethin'?
**Blue**
It drives itself, boy. This here is a gasoline, internal com-bustion six banger. Don't need no team a horses.
> *He pulls out a can of beans and walks around to* CISCO.

**Cisco**
I'll be damned. And this here is what ya' guide it with, I'll bet.
**Blue**
You got it. Here. There's a can opener in the glove com-partment.
**Cisco**
What's that?
**Blue**
That little door over there. Ya' just push the button and she flaps open.
**Cisco**
I'll be damned. Keep gloves in there, do ya'?
> *He opens the glove compartment and takes out a can opener and some other junk.*

**Blue**
Here, ya' better let me handle it for ya'.
> BLUE *takes the can and the can opener and opens the can of beans.*

**Cisco**
How fast can ya' go with one a these here?
**Blue**
Some of 'em'll do over a hundred mile an hour.
**Cisco**
What's that mean, Blue?
**Blue**
That means in an hour's time if you keep yer boot stomped down on that pedal you'll have covered a hundred mile a territory.
**Cisco**
Whooeee! Sure beats hell out of a quarter horse, don't it?

**Blue**
You better believe it.
**Cisco**
What's these buttons for?
> *He pulls a button and the headlights go on.*

**Blue**
Don't pull that! Push that back in. You want the fuzz down on our necks?
> CISCO *pushes the button back in and the lights go out.*

I just get the damn battery charged so's I can listen to a little radio and you wanna go and run the damn thing down again. Here's yer beans.
> *He hands* CISCO *the can of beans.*

**Cisco**
Thanks, boy. How come yer so scared a' the law all of a sudden?
**Blue**
It ain't so sudden as all that. I'm goin' on a hundred and twenty years old now. Thanks to modern medicine.
**Cisco**
That a fact? Sure kept yerself fit, Blue.
**Blue**
Well, you live on the lam like I have for a while and you gotta keep yer wits about ya'.
**Cisco**
What's this radio thing yer talking about?
**Blue**
That second knob on yer right. Just turn it a click. It's already set up for Moon Channel.
> CISCO *turns the radio on. Rock and Roll or news or any random radio station comes on soft. It should be a real radio and not a tape.*

**Cisco**
I'll be damned.
**Blue**
Just keep it soft.
**Cisco**
Where's it comin' from, Blue?

**Blue**

Up there. They got a station up there now.

> *He points to the moon.*

**Cisco**

The moon? Yer pullin' my leg.

**Blue**

Things've changed since you was last here, boy.

**Cisco**

How'd they get up there?

**Blue**

Rocket ship. Damndest thing ya' ever did see. Taller than a twenty story office building.

**Cisco**

How'd they get back?

**Blue**

Come right down plop in the ocean. Some of 'em stay up there, though. Don't know what they all do. I've heard tell they travel to Mars and Venus, different planets like that.

**Cisco**

All in a rocket ship thing?

**Blue**

Yep.

**Cisco**

Don't they like it down here no more?

**Blue**

The earth's gettin' cramped, boy. There's lots more people now. They're lookin' for new territory to spread out to. I hear tell they've sent prisoners up there too. 'Stead a sendin' 'em to jail. They don't hang no one no more. Just strand 'em high and dry on a planet somewheres in space. Probably where this critter come from.

**Cisco**

Wonder what's keepin' Sycamore.

**Blue**

What makes ya' so sure he's comin'?

**Cisco**

Has to. Same as me. He's been summoned up.

**Blue**

How's that work?

**Cisco**

Some voice wakes ya' up. I don't know. Just like you been sleepin' or somethin'. 'Fore you know it yer movin' and walkin' and talkin' just like always. Hard to get used to at first. Anyhow I'm glad I'm back.

**Blue**

Me too, boy. Sure gets lonely on yer own all the time.

**Cisco**

Well, before you know it we'll be back together just like old times. Robbin', rapin' and killin'.

**Blue**

Yeah boy!

> *A drunken high school cheerleader kid comes on yelling. He has a blond crewcut and a long cheerleader's sweater with a huge "A" printed on it. He holds a huge megaphone to his lips. His pants are pulled down around his ankles. His legs are red and bleeding and look as though they've been whipped with a belt. He has white tennis shoes on. He yells through the megaphone to an unseen gang of a rival high school in the distance behind the audience. He doesn't notice BLUE and CISCO.*

**Kid**

You motherfuckers are dead! You're as good as dead! Just wait till Friday night! We're going to wipe your asses off the map! There won't even be an Arcadia High left! You think you're all so fuckin' bitchin' just 'cause your Daddies are rich! Just 'cause your old man gives you a fuckin' full blown Corvette for Christmas and a credit card! You think your girls are so tough looking! They're fucking dogs! I wouldn't fuck an Arcadia girl if she bled out her ass hole! You punk faggots shouldn't even be in the same league as us! The Rio Hondo belongs to us! You're gonna go fucking scoreless Friday night and I'm gonna be right there cheering and seeing it all happen! Then we're gonna burn your fucking grandstand to the ground! Right to the fucking ground! Then we're gonna

burn a huge "A" for Azusa right in the middle of your fucking field. Right on the fifty yard line!
*He wheels around and faces* BLUE *and* CISCO.
What're you looking at? You think it's funny or something? What the fuck are you looking at? You wanna make something out of it? You wanna put your money where your mouth is? Come on! Come on! Try me! You think I'm funny looking? Come on!

**Blue**
I don't know, Cisco. This used to be a quiet little highway.

**Kid**
What'd you say, old man? What'd you say? I'll kill you if you say one more word! I'll fucking kill you!

**Cisco**
Better watch that kinda tongue, boy. This here's my brother Blue yer talkin' at.

**Kid**
What're you, some hippie creep? I can smell you all the way over here! I'll kill you too! I'll kill both of you!

**Cisco**
Better pull yer pants up and head home, boy.

**Kid**
Don't tell me what to do, you commie faggot! I'll fucking kill you!
*He takes a leap toward* CISCO. CISCO *draws his pistol lightning fast. The* KID *stops still.*

**Cisco**
Now look, boy. I ain't in the habit of shootin' down unarmed infants, but yer startin' to grate on me. Now git home before this thing goes off.
*The* KID *crumples to the ground sobbing.*

**Kid**
I can't! It's too late now. They grabbed me. Right after the rally. They got me and took me up Lookout Point and whipped me with a belt. They tried to paint my balls black but I wouldn't let them. I fought. I kicked. They stuck a Tampax up me. Right up me. I tried to stop them. I yelled.

There were some cars. A couple cars. Girls making out with the fullback and the quarterback. But they turned their lights on and left. They could've helped. At least they could have helped me. I cheered for them plenty of times. Plenty of games. The least they could've done— Just because I couldn't make second string. I could've played Junior Varsity but I decided to be a cheerleader instead. They could've helped me. The least they could've done.

**Cisco**

O.K. O.K. Why don't ya' just go home now and sleep it off.

**Kid**

I can't! It's too late. My old man'll beat the shit out of me. It's after two. He won't let me use the car for a month. I can't go home. Let me stay here. Please. Let me. Please.

**Blue**

Might as well. What's one more looney.

**Cisco**

We got business to set straight here, Blue.

**Blue**

He won't get in the way. Let him stay.

**Cisco**

All right. But keep to yerself over in the corner there.

**Kid**

Thanks.

> The KID *stands up and moves upstage left.*

**Cisco**

And pull yer pants up, fer Christ's sake.

**Kid**

It stings too bad.

**Cisco**

All right.

> The KID *throws down his megaphone and starts stomping on it violently.*

**Kid**

I'm never going to lead another cheer! Never! Not for them or anybody else! Never! Never! Never! Never! Never! Never! Never! Never! Never!

**Blue**
Atta boy. Get it out a yer system.
**Kid**
I'll just stay over near the drainage ditch there. I won't get in your way. I promise.
**Cisco**
Good.
**Kid**
If those Arcadia guys come by here don't tell them where I am, O.K.?
**Cisco**
O.K.

> *The* KID *turns to go off left then stops.*

**Kid**
Oh, would you mind waking me up in the morning? I don't usually get up too easy.
**Blue**
Don't worry, you'll hear the traffic.
**Kid**
Thanks.
**Blue**
Sweet dreams, boy.

> *The* KID *goes off.*

**Cisco**
Boy, howdy, what'd I miss all them years?
**Blue**
A whole lot, Cisco. A whole lot. Things change over night now. One day there's a President, the next day he gets shot, the next day the guy what shot him gets shot.
**Cisco**
No foolin'.
**Blue**
Next day they outlaw guns and replace 'em with nerve gas. Stuff can turn a full grown man into a blithering fool. Then they change the government from Capitalism to Socialism because the government's afraid of a full blown

insurrection. Then they have a revolution anyhow and things stay just like they was.

> WILLIE *rolls over and speaks on his back lying down.*

**Willie**

Cisco?

**Cisco**

That's me.

**Willie**

You made it. Good. Sycamore here yet?

**Cisco**

Not yet. Should be soon though.

> WILLIE *sits up.*

**Blue**

You feelin' better now, boy? That was some awful fit ya' had there.

**Willie**

Get prepared to see worse.

**Blue**

Why? You plannin' on flippin' out some more?

**Willie**

In Nogoland there's men walking around with their brains eaten out, skinless, eyes turned inside out, frozen in pictures of terror. Men walking day and night like dogs on the end of a leash. You'd be happy if the worst you saw there was "flipping out," as you say.

**Cisco**

What's the scoop, Willie?

**Blue**

How'd you know his name?

**Willie**

Long before we turned human, the magicians introduced us to the mysteries of telepathy, Blue. Your brother is able to know and understand things that he himself won't have the answers to.

**Blue**

Well, how 'bout me? Why don't ya clue me in on a few secrets?

**Willie**
It will take time. First of all you must undergo temporal rearrangement.
**Blue**
I don't get ya'.
**Cisco**
Yeah. Keep it simple, Willie.
**Willie**
Your brain has undergone cell breakdown with age and time, Blue. We have to regroup your temporal field to make you young enough to again become sensitive to telepathic and extrasensory reception.
**Blue**
Yer gonna make me young?
**Willie**
That's right.
**Cisco**
How 'bout that.
**Blue**
I don't exactly know if I go fer that idea. I been on a long hard road fer so long now it feels kinda good to know it's drawin' to a close. Now ya want me to go through it all over again?
**Willie**
Whenever you want it, the scheme can be reversed back to your normal earth age. But for now we must transform you, for it's the only hope for the prisoners of Nogoland.
**Blue**
Who are these dudes exactly? I don't even know if I like 'em yet.
**Willie**
People, like you and me but with a strange history and stranger powers. These powers could work for the good of mankind if allowed to unfold into their natural creativity. But if they continue as they are they will surely work for evil, or, worse, they will turn it on themselves and commit a horrible mass suicide that may destroy the universe.

**Blue**
Well, you seem like a decent enough Joe. What've I got to lose?
**Willie**
Fine.
**Cisco**
Good boy.
**Blue**
How do I start?
**Cisco**
Sit down here in front of me.
>WILLIE *sits with his feet out.*
**Blue**
Right here? Like this?
>BLUE *sits with his feet out facing* WILLIE.
**Willie**
That's right. Now push your feet against the soles of my feet. Real hard.
**Blue**
Like this?
>BLUE *presses his feet against* WILLIE's.
**Willie**
Press hard. Now grab my hands and squeeze.
>BLUE *follows* WILLIE's *directions.*
**Blue**
This ain't gonna hurt, is it?
**Willie**
Not a bit. You'll feel an interior shrinkage as your organs rearrange themselves and grow stronger, but don't panic. Just push with your feet and grip my hands firmly.
**Blue**
O.K.
**Cisco**
Hang on, Blue. Yer half way home.
>WILLIE *goes into another seizure but different this time. It's as though thousands of electric volts were being transmitted from* WILLIE *to* BLUE. *It should look like waves of shock being transformed. First* WILLIE *trembles and shakes vio-*

> *lently, then* BLUE. BLUE *gradually becomes younger until at the end he is a young man of about thirty.*

**Willie**

The truth of the spinning fire wheel! Steel brings you close! Strength in the steel! Strengthen! Electric smoking man power! The strength of a man! Power in the man! Tower of power! Texaco sucks! Texas man! Longhorn panhandle tough cowboy leather man! Send him home! Where the buffalo roam! It's daytime! It's bright day! Truth in the sun! Sun play! Mexican silver stud! Proud of his pride! Proud guy! Tall and lean and mean! Look out, Tuba City! Look out, down and out crumpled up muffled old bad guy! Here's screaming new blood! A flood of new blood screaming straight to your raggedy heart! Churning new blood flooding your mind up! Sending you zig zag straight to your heart! Aaaaaaaah! Gyrode screen! The Hand! The Hand's got me, Blue! The Hand!

**Blue**

Hang on, Willie. I'll see ya' through it.

> BLUE *grips* WILLIE's *hands tighter and pushes hard with his legs as* WILLIE *twists and grimaces trying to ward off the hand.*

**Willie**

No! No! Diminish laser count! Aaaaaah!

**Cisco**

Hang on, Blue! Don't let him go!

**Willie**

My brain! It's squeezing my brain!

**Blue**

Hold his head, Cisco! Grab his head!

> CISCO *puts both hands on* WILLIE's *head and presses down.*

**Willie**

Gama build up! System burn! Burning! Cell damage to block unit! Can't see! Can't see! They've smoked it good this time! Black wire smoke burn! There's a fire in code D! Disorient power pack! Aaaaaaaaaaah! Fading!

> *He shakes violently, then goes limp and unconscious as before.* CISCO *lowers his head to the ground as* BLUE *releases his grip.* BLUE *is now much younger than before. He stands.*

**Cisco**

Poor devil.

**Blue**

He'll be all right in a little while. The same thing happened
to him before you came. Anyway, it worked.

**Cisco**

What?

**Blue**

I'm young. Least I feel young. I still know it's me and
everything but I feel much stronger. Tough, like I used
to be.

**Cisco**

Hot damn! We're getting close now, Blue. It won't be long.

> BLUE *lets out a yell, takes a run across the stage and does
> a somersault.*

How 'bout that.

> CISCO *takes a run and does a somersault right next to* BLUE.
> BLUE *stands and starts singing "Rock Around The Clock."*
> CISCO *stands and joins him, dancing around and doing the
> twist and all that jive.*

**Cisco & Blue**

One for the money. Two for the show. Three to get ready.
Now go man go. We're gonna rock around the clock tonight. We're gonna rock, rock, rock until the broad daylight. We're gonna rock, gonna rock around the clock. . . .

> SYCAMORE MORPHAN *appears opposite them. They freeze.*
> SYCAMORE'S *very tall and slick. Dressed like Bat Master-
> son with black tails, black hat, black vest, white shirt with
> ruffled cuffs and diamond cuff links, black boots, black
> leather gloves and black cane with a diamond-studded
> handle and a pearl-handled revolver tied down to his hip in
> a black holster. He just stands staring at his two brothers.*

**Blue**

Sycamore.

**Cisco**

Hey, boy. Where you been? We been waitin' and waitin'.

> SYCAMORE *sidles over to* WILLIE *and pokes him with his
> cane.*

**Blue**

Thought you was probably lost or somethin'.

**Cisco**

Yeah. Don't know why we'd figure that though, since you know the trails better than any of us.

> *Uneasy silence as* SYCAMORE *moves to the Chevy and pokes it with his cane, scanning the area with his eyes. He is cold and mean. He reaches in the car and turns the radio off with a sharp snap.*

**Blue**

Sure is good to see us all back together again, though. Boy howdy, how long's it been, anyhow?

**Cisco**

Must be goin' on a hundred some-odd years, I'll bet.

**Blue**

Sure. Must be that. At least a hundred.

**Cisco**

Yer lookin' mighty fit, Sycamore. Just like old times.

> SYCAMORE *turns to them swinging his cane.*

**Sycamore**

Was there some specific reason behind choosing a rendezvous point right on the open highway?

**Blue**

This here's Azusa, Sycamore. "Everything from A to Z in the USA." Nothing hardly but rock quarries and cement factories here. All the traffic dies down at night on account of most of the vehicles is trucks carrying gravel and they don't work at night.

**Sycamore**

The sun don't rise on Azusa, huh.

**Blue**

Well, sure. But we'll be out a here by then.

**Cisco**

Yeah, we should be long gone by mornin'.

**Sycamore**

I guess you boys know exactly where you're goin', then, and how you're gettin' there.

**Cisco**

Well, not exactly. But Willie's gotta set us straight soon as he comes to.

**Sycamore**
I reckon he's got you all set up with enough guns and provisions, then, huh.

**Blue**
Hadn't thought a' that one.

**Cisco**
Well, we all got guns, ain't we? I got mine.
>    SYCAMORE *takes out a cheroot and lights it.*

**Sycamore**
We just meet 'em in the street, then, huh? Like old times. A showdown.

**Cisco**
Yeah, why not?

**Blue**
I see what Sycamore's drivin' at, Cisco. There's only three of us with pistols against hundreds, maybe thousands.

**Cisco**
So what. We used to bring a whole town to a standstill just by ridin' in. They used to roll out the carpet for the Morphan brothers.

**Blue**
This ain't a town Willie's talkin' about, it's a whole country, maybe even a whole planet. We ain't in the movies, ya' know.

**Cisco**
So what do you suggest we do?

**Blue**
Round up some more men maybe.

**Cisco**
Why don't we wake Willie up and ask him.

**Sycamore**
I say we forget it.
>    *A pause as they both look at* SYCAMORE.

**Blue**
The whole thing?

**Sycamore**
Why not? We don't stand a chance of freeing those baboons.
**Blue**
But they ain't baboons any more, Sycamore. They're human beings just like us.
**Cisco**
Yeah.
**Sycamore**
So what?
**Blue**
They're bein' tortured and stuff. Brainwashed or somethin'. Experimented on.
**Sycamore**
What's that got to do with us? We're free now. We been brought back to life. What do you want to throw it away for a bunch of baboons? Look, I say we split up, go our different ways and lay low for a while. Then we meet up again in Tuba City or somewhere on the North Platte. That way it'll give us time to think things over.
**Cisco**
What things?
**Sycamore**
Reorganizing the gang, you pinhead. The Morphan brothers ride again, except this time in a whole different century. This time we don't make no mistakes. We stick to trains and forget about banks and post offices.
**Blue**
There ain't no trains no more, Sycamore. Just planes and hovercrafts and such like.
**Sycamore**
What're you talkin' about?
**Blue**
There ain't no trains to rob no more. Besides, we can't ditch Willie like that. He just give me back my youth. I can't go walkin' out on him.
**Sycamore**
No trains?

**Cisco**
Yeah, I feel kinda' bad about that too. I wouldn't even be here if it weren't for him. You neither, Sycamore.

**Sycamore**
No trains.

**Blue**
I say we stay and see it through.

      WILLIE *comes to.*

**Willie**
It's up to you. What Sycamore says is true. Why should you feel responsible for some species of hybrid in another galaxy? You could stay here and be free. Live like you want to.

**Cisco**
You mean you wouldn't mind if we took off on ya'?

**Willie**
I can't force you to help us. It must be left to your own conscience. All I can do is to try to persuade you to come.

**Sycamore**
No trains.

**Blue**
Oh, this here's my brother Sycamore, Willie.

**Willie**
I know. I'm happy you came.

**Sycamore**
They got trains where you come from?

**Willie**
They used to have a system underground but it's long been made obsolete.

**Sycamore**
It's still there though?

**Willie**
Yes. As far as I know.

**Sycamore**
And it connects to all the parts of the city where these prisoners are?

**Willie**
Yes. I think it must. Throughout the whole planet, I think.

**Blue**
What you gettin' at, Sycamore?

**Sycamore**
Sounds to me like it could be used as an escape route.

**Cisco**
Then we're goin' then! Waaaahoooo! Attaboy, Sycamore!
I always knew ya' had a soft spot.

**Sycamore**
Well, if there's no trains here we might as well go there.

**Blue**
Hot dog!

**Willie**
Good. Let me show you a plan of Nogoland.

> WILLIE *stands and draws a huge map with his finger on the
> floor of the stage. As he indicates lines different colored lines
> of light appear on the floor as though they emanated from the
> tip of his finger. The other three watch as* WILLIE *describes
> Nogoland and draws the map accordingly.*

In the Northeastern sector is the Capitol, as you would
say, contained in a transparent dome permitting tem-
perature and atmosphere control. It is here that the Silent
Ones conduct their affairs of state. Only members of the
High Commission and Sorcerer Chiefs are allowed pas-
sage to and from the Capitol. Over here in the South-
western sector are the Diamond Fields where slaves
work day and night under constant guard by the soldiers
of the Raven Cult.

**Blue**
Who're they?

**Willie**
Fierce morons cloaked in black capes. They ride on huge
black ravens which continually fly over the area, patrol-
ling and keeping a constant eye out for the possibility of
an uprising amongst the slaves. Here in the West are the
laboratories of the Sorcerers of the Nogo. Here is where
my friends are kept. They are also watched by Raven
guards but the control is not so heavy there since the

power of the Unseen Hand is believed to be security enough.

**Sycamore**
What's in the middle?

**Willie**
Huge refineries and industrial compounds for the process-ing of the diamonds. It is here that the biggest and best diamonds are culled out of the crop.

**Blue**
What do they do with them?

**Willie**
Each year a Great Game is played with the people of Zeron, a competition of some kind. The winner is allowed to extend the boundaries of his domain into the loser's territory and rule the people within that new area. The loser must also pay off the winner with certain secret information of magical knowledge.

**Sycamore**
What about the South?

**Willie**
A vast primitive region of swamps and lagoons. We must enter Nogoland by this route since we'll surely be spotted by Raven guards if we attempt to come in from the North.

**Blue**
What's up there?

**Willie**
Desert. Nothing. The sky never changes. No day and no night. No atmosphere of any kind. Not even craters to break up the landscape. We would surely be seen.

**Sycamore**
How do they get back and forth from these different areas?

**Willie**
Only certain chosen ones are allowed to travel at all. These do so by means of teleportation. They beam them-selves into a chosen area by displacing their bodies.

**Sycamore**

Does this underground railroad you're talkin' about go into the South there?

**Willie**

Just about. We'll have to be extra careful once we arrive there, though.

**Blue**

Why's that?

**Willie**

This region is inhabited by the Lagoon Baboon, another experiment on our race. He watches over the Lower Regions and is also controlled by the Hand.

**Sycamore**

Uh, don't anybody let on to it but we're being watched.

**Blue**

What do you mean?

**Sycamore**

Don't turn around. Act like we're still talkin' about the map. He's over behind the car. I'll try to circle around behind him.

**Cisco**

How ya' gonna do that without him seein' ya'?

**Sycamore**

I'll go off like I'm goin' to take a leak then come up behind him. You stay here and keep talkin'. Just act natural.

**Blue**

O.K.

**Cisco**

So ya' say this here Lagoon Baboon's an ornery critter, eh Willie?

**Willie**

Yes. Very ornery, as you say. He can eat three times his weight in human flesh in less time than it would take you to eat a donut.

**Sycamore**

Well listen, I gotta go see a man about a horse so why don't you fellas carry on here.

**Blue**
O.K., Sycamore. Don't get it caught in the zipper now.
> SYCAMORE *exits. The rest continue to act "natural."*

**Cisco**
Sounds to me like this Nogoland's a pretty depressing place. Don't they ever have no fun? No rodeos or nothin'?

**Blue**
Yeah. What about that, Willie?

**Willie**
Twice a year they hold tournaments where my people are pitted against beasts from other galaxies. Also robots and androids are programmed to fight my people in the Gaming Arena.

**Blue**
Where's that at?

**Willie**
Right here in the East.
> *He draws another area of light with his finger.*

Many of my people are slaughtered each year in the tournaments.

**Cisco**
Don't they ever win?

**Willie**
It has only happened once and the Silent Ones were so impressed and stunned that they allowed the man his freedom but kept him still under the control of the Hand.

**Blue**
Well, what happened to him? Where's he now?

**Willie**
Right here. It is me they set free.

**Cisco**
You? Hot dog! You must be a mean hombre, Willie.

**Blue**
But how come they let you go?

**Willie**
The Silent Ones believed I could not survive the South-land and the Lagoon Baboon. Plus they still had control

over me with the Hand. They thought if I was to return to my people I would cause trouble so rather than kill me they played another game.

> *Voice of the* KID *yelling from behind the car. He comes out into the open with his hands raised and his pants still down and* SYCAMORE *right behind him with his gun out.*

**Kid**

Wait a minute! Wait a minute! Please. I didn't mean to bother you. I just couldn't sleep and I heard you talking so I came over. I just wanted to listen.

**Sycamore**

He's heard the whole shootin' match.

**Cisco**

I told you once, boy. How come you didn't listen?

**Kid**

I know, but I can help you. I want to come with you.

**Sycamore**

I say we put a bullet through his head.

**Blue**

Now wait a minute, Sycamore.

**Willie**

What makes you say you could help us?

**Kid**

I know about that kind of fighting. I learned it in school.

**Sycamore**

Come on. He's seen our whole hand.

**Blue**

Hear him out.

**Kid**

Three things: Constant movement, absolute mistrust and eternal vigilance. Movement: that is, never stay put; never spend two nights in the same place; never stop moving from one place to another. Mistrust: at the beginning mistrust even your own shadow, friendly peasants, informants, guides, contacts; mistrust everything until you hold a liberated zone. Vigilance: constant guard duty, constant reconnaissance; establishment of a camp in a safe place and, above all, never sleep beneath a roof, never sleep in a house where you can be surrounded.

**Cisco**

I'll be damned.

**Willie**

And how does this apply to our mission? We go to free prisoners, not to start a revolution.

**Cisco**

Yeah.

**Kid**

The two are inseparable. Freedom and revolution are inextricably bound up. To free the oppressed you must get rid of the oppressor. This constitutes revolution. And the surest means to victory is guerrilla warfare. This has held true for hundreds of years.

**Willie**

Then you see no other way to liberate my people than to make war with the Silent Ones?

**Kid**

Exactly.

**Sycamore**

Keep those hands up.

**Cisco**

And pull up yer pants, fer Christ's sake.

> The KID *goes to pull up his pants.*

**Sycamore**

I told ya' to keep yer hands raised.

**Kid**

Well, I can't do both.

**Blue**

Let him pull up his pants, Sycamore.

**Sycamore**

This here is a spy in case you forgot. I say we plug him right here and now.

**Blue**

And I say we let him pull up his doggone pants!

**Cisco**
What do you say, Willie?
**Willie**
I have come to find any means possible to free my people.
If he has information we should listen.
**Sycamore**
O.K. But keep yer hands high, mister.
> *The* KID *talks with his hands raised and his pants down. The others listen.*
**Kid**
First of all you need more men. A guerrilla unit should be small but four or five is not enough to be fully effective.
**Blue**
Well, let's see, there's Red Diamond.
**Cisco**
And Slim and Shadow. We could get them easy.
**Sycamore**
What about Fatback?
**Cisco**
Yeah. And then there's Sloe Gin Martin, Cat Man Kelly, Booger Montgomery, the Mouse, Mojo Moses—
**Kid**
That's enough. Ten to fifteen is all you'll need in the initial stages. It's important to remember that what you're organizing is more than a gang of bandits. Guerrilla warfare is a war of the masses, a war of the people. The guerrilla band is an armed nucleus, the fighting vanguard of the people. It draws its great force from the mass of the people themselves. Bandit gangs have all the characteristics of a guerrilla army, homogeneity, respect for the leader, valor, knowledge of the ground and often even good understanding of the tactics to be employed. The only thing missing is support of the people and inevitably these gangs are captured and exterminated by the public force.
**Willie**
But the people you speak of, the masses, in this case are all held prisoner.

**Kid**

Then you must liberate a few for reinforcements.

**Blue**

How?

**Kid**

Hit and run, wait, lie in ambush, again hit and run, and thus repeatedly, without giving any rest to the enemy. The blows should be continuous. The enemy ought not to be allowed to sleep. At every moment the impression ought to be created that he is surrounded by a complete circle.

**Sycamore**

Keep those hands high.

**Willie**

Go on.

**Kid**

Acts of sabotage are very important. It is necessary to distinguish between sabotage and terrorism, a measure that is generally ineffective and indiscriminate in its results, since it often makes victims of innocent people and destroys a large number of lives that would be valuable to the revolution. Sabotage should be of two types: sabotage on a national scale against determined objectives, and local sabotage against lines of combat. Sabotage on a national scale should be aimed principally at destroying communications. The guerrilla is a night combatant. He thrives in the dark, while the enemy is afraid of the dark. He must be cunning and able to march unnoticed to the place of attack, across plains or mountains, and then fall upon the enemy, taking advantage of the factor of surprise. After causing panic by this surprise he should launch himself into the fight implacably without permitting a single weakness in his companions and taking advantage of every sign of weakness in the enemy. Striking like a tornado, destroying all, giving no quarter unless the tactical circumstances call for it, judging those who must be judged, sowing panic among the enemy, he nevertheless treats defenseless prisoners benevolently and shows respect for the dead.

**Blue**

Now I say we let him pull his pants up.

**Cisco**

Yeah, let him, Sycamore. What the hell.

**Sycamore**

All right. Pull 'em up but nice and slow.

> The KID *very slowly bends down and goes to pull up his pants. He gets them halfway up then suddenly kicks* SYCA-MORE *in the balls and grabs his gun.* SYCAMORE *falls on the ground holding his crotch and groaning. The* KID *holds the gun on all of them.*

**Cisco**

What the hell!

**Kid**

All right! Now up, all of you! Get your hands up! Don't try anything or I'll shoot. Honest I will. All I'll have to tell the cops is I caught a bunch of subversives right in the act. They wouldn't think twice. In fact they'd probably call me a hero.

> *They all raise their hands.*

**Sycamore**

I told you! I told ya' we shoulda' killed the bastard.

**Kid**

He's right, you know.

**Blue**

Well, you sure disappointed me, boy.

**Kid**

Why? What do I owe you?

**Blue**

Here I thought you was gonna lead us on to victory and all.

**Cisco**

Yeah, me too. The way you was talkin'. . . .

**Kid**

Shut up! Don't say anything more or I'll kill all of you! I mean it.

**Cisco**
Ya' really ought to pull yer pants up though. It don't look right.

**Kid**
Shut up!

**Cisco**
I mean we're your prisoners and you got yer pants pulled down like yer about to get whooped or something.

> The KID *struggles to pull up his pants with one hand while he holds the gun on them with the other. He gets them up around his waist and hangs on to them with one hand.*

**Kid**
You better shut up!

**Willie**
Don't tease him.

**Cisco**
That's right. He's had a rough night.

**Blue**
What you gonna' do now, boy? How ya' gonna go fer help?

**Kid**
We'll wait until morning. There'll be plenty of trucks.

**Blue**
Yer gonna' tell 'em you captured a bunch a' subversives single handed, huh?

**Kid**
That's right! And everything else too. How you were planning to take over Azusa.

> SYCAMORE *starts laughing hysterically, then screams with pain, then back to laughter. The others join in laughing except for* WILLIE, *who watches.*

**Sycamore**
Azusa!

**Cisco**
That's a good one! "Everything from A to Z in the USA." Yeah boy!

**Kid**

*In the background the old "C" "A" "F" "G" Rock and Roll chords are played to the* KID's *speech.*

Shut up! Shut up! I'll kill you all! I'll kill you! This is my home! Don't make fun of my home. I was born and raised here and I'll die here! I love it! That's something you can't understand! I love Azusa! I love the foothills and the drive in movies and the bowling alleys and the football games and the drag races and the girls and the donut shop and the High School and the Junior College and the outdoor track meets and the parades and the Junior Chamber of Commerce and the Key Club and the Letterman's Club and the Kiwanis and the Safeway Shopping Center and the freeway and the pool hall and the Bank of America and the Post Office and the Presbyterian

*They laugh louder and louder as* KID *keeps on.*

church and the Laundromat and the liquor store and the miniature golf course and Lookout Point and the YMCA and the Glee Club and the basketball games and the sock hop and graduation and the prom and the cafeteria and the principal's office and Chemistry class and the county fair and peanut· butter and jelly sandwiches and the High School band and going steady and KFWB and white bucks and pegger pants and argyle socks and madras shorts and butch wax and Hobie boards and going to the beach and getting drunk and swearing and reading dirty books and smoking in the men's room and setting off cherry bombs and fixing up my car and my Mom, I love my Mom most of all. And you creeps aren't going to take that away from me. You're not going to take that away from me because I'll kill you first! I'll kill every one of you if it's the last thing I do!

*They all stop laughing.* WILLIE *goes into a trance, speaking a strange ancient language. The others watch.*

**Willie**

Od i gniht tsal eht sti fi uoy fo eno yreve llik lli. Tsrif ouy llik lli esuaceb em morf yawa taht ekat ot gniog ton eruoy.

Em morf yawa taht ekat ot gniog tnera speerc uoy dna.
Lla fo tsom mom ym evol i mom ym dna rac ym pu gnixif
dna sbmob yrrehc ffo gnittes dna moor . . .

**Kid**

Shut up, you! Shut up!

**Willie**

. . . snem eht ni gnikoms dna skoob ytrid gnidaer dna gni-
raews dna knurd gnitteg dna hcaeb eht ot gniog dna
sdraob eiboh dna xaw hctub dna strohs sardam dna skcos
elygra dna stnap reggep dna skcub etihw dna bwfk
dna . . .

> The KID *fires the pistol into* WILLIE *but* WILLIE *keeps on
> speaking and getting very weird.*

. . . ydaets gniog dna dnab loohcs hgih eht dna sehciw-
dnas yllej dna rettub tunaep dna riaf ytnuoc eht dna ssalc
yrtsimehc . . .

**Kid**

Shut up!

> The KID *fires again.* WILLIE *keeps on.*

**Willie**

. . . dna eciffo slapicnirp eht dna airetefac eht dna morp
eht dna noitaudarg dna poh kcos eht dna semag . . .

> The KID *empties the gun into* WILLIE *but* WILLIE *continues,
> accumulating incredible power from the language he
> speaks.*

. . . llabteksab eht dna bulc eelg eht dna acmy eht dna
tniop tuokool dna esruoc flog erutainim eht dna erots
rouqil eht dna tamordnual eht dna hcruhc nairetybserp
eht dna eciffo tsop eht dna acirema fo knab eht dna llah
loop eht dna yaweerf eht dna retnec gnippohs yawefas
eht dna bulc snamrettel eht dna bulc yek eht dna ecrem-
moc fo rebmahc roinuj . . .

> The KID *screams and holds his hands to his ears. His whole
> body twitches and writhes as* WILLIE *did when the hand
> grabbed him.*

**Kid**

Stop it! Stop it! I can't—No! No more! Stop!

**Willie**

. . . eht dna sedarap eht dna steem kcart roodtuo eht dna egelloc roinuj eht dna loohcs hgih eht dna pohs tunod eht dna slrig eht dna secar gard eht dna semag llabtoof eht dna syella gnilwob eht dna seivom ni evird eht dna sllihtoof eht evol i . . .

**Kid**

No! No! My head! My brain! Stop it!

> *He falls to the ground holding his head and writhing, scream-ing for mercy.*

**Willie**

Asuza evol i. Dnatsrednu tnac uoy gnihtemos staht. Ti evol i. Ereh desiar dna nrob saw i. Emoh ym fo nuf ekam tnod. Emoh ym si siht. Uoy, llik lli. Lla noy llik lli. Pu tuhs! Pu tuhs! Free! Free! Free! Free! Free! Free!

> *WILLIE goes into an elated dance as the KID screams on the floor. Very gradually dayglo painted ping pong balls start to fall from the ceiling passing through black light as they fall and bouncing on the stage as WILLIE screams "Free" over and over again and dances.*

**Blue**

Willie! What's goin' on!

**Willie**

I have discovered their secret! The Hand is in my control! I have the Hand! We are free! Free! Free!

**Kid**

My brain! I can't stand it!

**Willie**

My people are free! Nogoland is exploding! The Silent Ones are dying! Look! Look at the sky!

> *As they look up at the sky more and more ping pong balls fall, dayglo strips of paper flutter to the ground. CISCO joins WILLIE in his dance and yells "free" with him. SYCAMORE and BLUE look at the sky. SYCAMORE takes off his hat and catches the balls and throws them up in the air. BLUE joins in.*

**Cisco**

Free! Free! Yipeee! Wahoooo! Alaman left and swing her low! Catch her on the backside and watch her glow!

**Blue**
Then we don't have to go to no other galaxy after all. We can stay right here!

**Sycamore**
We're free! Free!

**Kid**
No! My brain!

**Willie**
It was all in my brain the whole time. In my mind. The ancient language of the Nogo. Right in my brain. I've destroyed them by breaking free of the Hand. They have no control. We can do what we want! We're free to do what we want.

**Blue**
Let's have us a party, Willie.

**Cisco**
Sure, we'll invite the old gang. You can call them all back, Willie. You've got the power.

**Willie**
So have you. Do it yourself. Do whatever you want. I've got to leave.

**Blue**
How come?

**Sycamore**
You just got here, I thought.

**Willie**
My people need me now more than ever. Now we can start to build our own world.

**Blue**
What's a' matter with this one?

**Willie**
I am a visitor here. I came for help. This is your world. Do what you want with it.

**Cisco**
But we're strangers too. We're lost, Willie.

**Willie**
Good luck.

**Blue**
Wait!

> WILLIE *exits. The* KID *is frozen in an attitude of terror.*

**Sycamore**
Well of all the damn nerve. He just used us.

**Cisco**
What're we gonna' do now?

**Blue**
Anything.

**Cisco**
Stop talkin' like him, dammit. We're in some pickle, Blue. It's gonna' be mornin' and here we are stuck in some other century in some hick town called Azusa somewheres.

**Blue**
"Everything from A to Z in the USA." That's us all right.

**Cisco**
Stop saying that over and over all the time!

**Sycamore**
What do you mean, "That's us all right"?

**Blue**
Now they got us thrown in to boot.

**Cisco**
And I ain't so sure they're gonna go fer the idea. He sure didn't.

**Sycamore**
What're we gonna do with him anyway?

**Cisco**
I say we plug him.

**Blue**
He's free like us.

**Sycamore**
Free to kill us, ya' mean.

**Cisco**
Yeah, or turn us in to the law.

**Blue**
If you waste him there's gonna be a dozen more to take his place. Look at him. He's as good as dead anyway.

**Cisco**
He's right, Sycamore.

**Sycamore**
I don't know. Can't seem to think straight. Who runs this town anyhow? That's the dude to go to. Straight to the top.

**Blue**
The mayor?

**Sycamore**
The mayor.

**Blue**
He runs the cops. The governor runs the mayor.

**Sycamore**
The governor. What's his name?

**Blue**
Congress runs the governor. President runs the Congress.

**Sycamore**
What's his name? We gotta get outa' this.

**Cisco**
We could hide in the drainage ditch.

**Sycamore**
Yeah, we could sit it out. We ain't done nothin' wrong.

**Cisco**
We could change our names. Get a haircut, some new threads. Blend right in.

**Sycamore**
That's it. That's the ticket. I could get me an office job easy enough.

**Cisco**
Sure. Western Union. Pacific Gas and Electric. Plenty of places.

**Sycamore**
Settle down with a nice little pension. Get me a car maybe.

**Cisco**
Yeah boy. And one a' them lawnmowers ya' sit on like a tractor.
**Sycamore**
Sure. We could fit right into the scheme a' things. Don't have to bust our balls for nobody. What do ya' say, Blue?
**Blue**
Whatever you boys want. I'm gonna be long gone by mornin'.
**Cisco**
What do you mean, Blue?
**Blue**
I'm leavin'. I been hangin' around this dump fer twenty years. Seems about time to get the lead out.
> *He moves toward the car and pulls the suitcase out of the back seat.*
**Cisco**
But where you gonna go? What you gonna do?
**Blue**
I'll answer them questions when they come up. Right now I just gotta move. That's all I know.
**Cisco**
Well, let me come with ya' then. Please, Blue.
**Blue**
All right.
**Cisco**
Sycamore? You comin'? We oughta' stick together since we're brothers and all.
**Sycamore**
Naw, thanks anyway. Think I'll stay awhile.
**Cisco**
All right. So long then.
**Blue**
Sorry it didn't work out like you want, Syc. . . .
**Sycamore**
Don't matter. Seemed unreal from the start anyhow.
**Blue**
Yeah. I know what you mean.

**Sycamore**

You boys go ahead on and take care, ya' hear. Don't worry about me.

**Cisco**

Good luck, Syc.

**Sycamore**

Yeah. You too.

**Blue**

Peace.

> BLUE *and* CISCO *exit.* SYCAMORE *looks down at the* KID, *still frozen grotesquely. He stares at the* KID's *face and slowly becomes older and older just with his body. He turns to the Chevy and talks to an imaginary driver as* BLUE *did in the beginning.*

**Sycamore**

> *In ancient voice.*

Well now. Well. Sure is decent of ya' stoppin' so late of an evenin' fer an old wreck like me. Yes sir. Mighty decent. Cars get to rollin' by here, eighty, ninety, a hundred mile an hour. Don't even see the landscape. Just a blur. Just a blue blur. Can't figure it. Wouldn't hardly call it a vacation now, would ya'. Screamin' out to Desert Hot Springs, back to Napa Valley. Don't even see the country. Not to speak of. Most folks is too scared, I guess. That's what it mounts up to. A certain terrorism in the air. A night terror. That's what's got 'em all locked up goin' so fast they can't see. Me, I'm slow by nature. I got nothin' agin' speed now, mind ya'. I've done plenty a speed in my time to know the taste good and well. Speed's a pleasure. Yes sir. Naw, that ain't it. Mind if I grab yer back seat here so's I can curl up? Feet are awful dogged. Good. Mighty kind. Mighty kind.

> *He opens the door of the Chevy and slowly climbs in the back seat. The lights fade slowly as he gradually disappears in the back while he talks.*

It's just a hankerin' to take stock a' things. A man's gotta be still long enough to figure out his next move. Know what I mean? Like in checkers, fer example. Can't just plunge in. Gotta make plans. Figure out yer moves. Make sure they're yer own moves and not someone else's. That's the great thing about this country, ya' know. The fact that you can make yer own moves in yer own time without some guy behind the scenes pullin' the switches on ya'. May be a far cry from bein' free, but it sure comes closer than most anything I've seen. Me, I don't yearn fer much any more but to live out my life with a little peace and quiet. I done my bit, God knows. God knows that much. There comes a time to let things by. Just let 'em go by. Let the world alone. It'll take care of itself. Just let it be.

> As SYCAMORE *disappears the lights fade out. Guitar music accompanies ending speech.*

## THE END

# Forensic & the Navigators

FORENSIC & THE NAVIGATORS was first produced at the Theatre Genesis in December 1967. The cast appeared in the following order:

*Forensic* ............................. Bob Schlee
*Emmet* ............................... Lee Kissman
*Oolan* ..................... O-Lan Johnson-Shepard
*1st Exterminator* ...................... Walter Hadler
*2nd Exterminator* .................... Beeson Carrol

This production was directed by Ralph Cook.

It was subsequently presented by Albert Poland at the Astor Place Theatre on April 1, 1970 with the following cast:

*Forensic* ........................... Peter Maloney
*Emmet* ............................. David Clennon
*Oolan* ..................... O-Lan Johnson-Shepard
*1st Exterminator* ...................... Tom Rosica
*2nd Exterminator* ...................... Ron Abbott

This production was directed by Jeff Bleckner.

# Scene:

*Black space. A small table center stage with a long white linen tablecloth that goes almost to the floor. An old-fashioned oil lamp in the center of the table. Two office-type swivel chairs at opposite ends of the table facing each other. FORENSIC sits in the stage right chair with a note pad and pen in front of him. He has long blond hair, a brown cowboy hat, a long red scarf, a black leather vest, jeans and moccasins. EMMET sits at the other end of the table with a small portable typewriter in front of him with paper in it. He has long black hair, a green Cherokee head band, beads around his neck, a serape, jeans and cowboy boots. An elaborate Indian peace pipe sits in the center of the table in a large glass ash tray. The stage is black. Sound of EMMET's typewriter clacking. Silence. Whole cast sing in the dark.*

**Whole Cast**

We gonna be born again. Oh Lord
We gonna get born again. Good Lord.
We gonna be born again.
Lord have mercy now.

> We gonna be saved tonight. Oh Lord.
> We gonna get saved tonight. Good Lord.
> We gonna be saved tonight.
> Lord have mercy now.
> *They sing both verses three times through, then stop short. Silence. Sound of* EMMET's *typewriter. The oil lamp slowly glows and becomes brighter. The light comes up full. As the characters become visible, they both relax from their writing and lean back in the chairs like executives. They stare at each other.*

**Forensic**

Where's that woman, Emmet? Ya can't count on her to get ya a hot meal on the table 'afore six A.M., then could ya tell me what kinda good is she? Tell me that one, Emmet.

> EMMET *just stares at* FORENSIC, *then begins to type.*

So as far as you're concerned we're really cutting out of here. I take it that that's the story so far. Do I take it right, Emmet? Right or wrong? Do I take it right or wrong?

> *He stands and slams his fist on the table.* EMMET *stops typing and looks at* FORENSIC.

Boy, I'll cut you down! Answer me right or wrong!

**Emmet**

If you have to be stubborn, do it outside, Forensic. I'm writing a letter.

**Forensic**

Who to then? Tell me that much. Jesus, I feel so far out of what's going on since you and everyone else decides we ain't goin' through with a whole plan that's been goin' on since we was ten years old.

**Emmet**

Sit.

> FORENSIC *sits.*

Now, I'm writing to my mother and for me to do that I have to have my wits. Would you like a smoke?

**Forensic**

Your mother. Jesus. All right. I'll light it.

> *He picks up the peace pipe and lights it.*

**Emmet**
It's no good being disappointed, Forensic. We've been through that. We have to just lay low for a while. We need you a lot so don't go feeling left out of things. Right now we have to take care of certain business. We have to transfer the guns and the equipment. We have to individually escape. We have to be quiet. We have to do these things before we make any moves. If we make any other moves we're screwed and that's the end of that. We have to switch our sensibilities so that we're not even pretending. So that we are transformed for a time and see no difference in the way we are from the way we were. We have to believe ourselves.

**Forensic**
Here.
> *He hands the pipe to* EMMET, *who smokes it.*

It's just chicken, Emmet, and you know it. It's downright yellow and cowardly. We could blow that whole place up in less time than it would take to go through a sensibility switch. Besides, there's people in there now who are really trapped for real. What about them? We're out here switching disguises while they only think of ways to escape. We could blow that whole motherfucker sky high and you know it.

**Emmet**
Here.
> *He hands the pipe to* FORENSIC, *who smokes.*

Don't talk like a dumb kid, Forensic. You got any idea whatsoever what this project looks like from the outside, objectively, without emotion? Why, it looks overwhelming, Forensic. It's a fucking desert fortress is what it amounts to. They've rebuilt it since the time of the Japanese, you know. It's not the same camp at all. New plumbing, double inlaid wire fencing that fronts a steel wall thirty feet high without doors.

**Forensic**

How do they get in, then, and what difference does the plumbing make?

**Emmet**

By helicopter and the plumbing difference is that since its reconstruction we have no idea what the design is underground, which makes internal explosions almost out of the question.

**Forensic**

Then bomb the mother fucker.

**Emmet**

And kill all the inmates. RIGHT! BOMB THE MOTHER FUCKER AND KILL ALL THE INMATES! THAT'S WHAT YOU'RE SAYING! THAT'S WHAT YOU'RE SAYING, FORENSIC! OUT OF MY SIGHT! GET OUT OF MY SIGHT! I DON'T WANT TO SEE YOU EVER AGAIN.

> *He stands and lunges toward FORENSIC as OOLAN enters wearing a white hospital gown such as is worn by the insane, and sandals on her feet. She holds a frying pan with a single pancake in it. She circles the table flipping the pancake and catching it in the pan.*

**Oolan**

You boys should have told me what hour it was getting to be. Why, my goodness sakes, I look at the clock and the time is getting to be way past the time for you boys' breakfast. And you both know how uptight the two of you get when breakfast isn't just exactly when you get the most hungry. So here it is. Hot and ready.

> *She flips the pancake onto the table. FORENSIC and EMMET stare at the pancake as OOLAN smiles. EMMET sits back in his chair. OOLAN picks up the pipe and smokes it.*

**Emmet**

How many times I gotta tell you I don't eat that buckwheat Aunt Jemima middle-class bullshit. I want Rice Krispies and nothing else. Is that clear?

**Forensic**

Get that pancake off the conference table, you stupid girl.

**Oolan**

Here.

> *She hands the pipe to* FORENSIC, *then picks up the pancake and eats it slowly as she watches them.*

**Forensic**

Emmet, you're as soft and flabby as you say your enemies are.

**Emmet**

You're pretty much of a shit yourself. Shit face.

> *A loud knock that sounds like somebody banging on a steel door with a sledge hammer.* EMMET *and* FORENSIC *stand suddenly and pull out small ray guns they have concealed in their crotches.* EMMET *motions to* OOLAN *to answer.*

**Oolan**

I can't, my mouth is full.

> *Another loud knock.* EMMET *motions again, more angry this time.* OOLAN *forces the pancake down and fixes her hair. She faces upstage and answers.*

Who is it? Just one moment, please.

> *Another loud knock.* EMMET *motions again, really mad.* OOLAN *crosses upstage.*

Yes. Hello. Who is it, please?

**Exterminator's Voice**

IT'S THE EXTERMINATOR, LADY!

> *She looks at* EMMET, *who waves his ray gun and shakes his head.*

**Oolan**

Um—we don't want any. Thank you anyway.

**Exterminator's Voice**

DON'T WANT ANY WHAT? IT'S THE EXTERMINATOR. OPEN UP!

**Oolan**

O.K. Wait just a second.

> *She turns to* EMMET *and shrugs her shoulders.* EMMET *and* FORENSIC *duck under the tablecloth and disappear. Another loud knock.*

Coming! Just hold tight.

> *Two huge men appear in the light. They are dressed like California Highway Patrolmen, with gold helmets, gas masks, khaki pants and shirts, badges, boots, gloves, and pistols.*

> *They carry large tanks on their backs with hose and nozzle attachments which they hold in their hands. They just stand there and look around the room.*

Um—we haven't had any rats here since last February, March, around in there.

**1st Exterminator**

Well, they told us to cover the place from top to bottom.

**2nd Exterminator**

You'll have to leave, ma'am.

**Oolan**

Fuck you. This is my home.

> EMMET'S VOICE *is heard from under the table.*

**Emmet's Voice**

Cool it, Oolan.

> *The* EXTERMINATORS *wander around, casing the joint.*

**Oolan**

Um—don't you think you had better check it out with your home office and see if you got the right place? I mean it would be awful if you got the wrong place. Don't you think? What do you think, fellas?

**1st Exterminator**

This is exactly the place, little girl.

**2nd Exterminator**

The table gives it away. Without the table or with the table in another place maybe it would be cause to call the home office. But with the table in the place it is and looking the way it does there is absolutely no doubt we have the right place.

> *They both turn upstage to adjust nozzles and synchronize watches. As they do this* FORENSIC *and* EMMET *lift the table from underneath and move it upstage right so the table looks as though it moves by itself.*

**1st Exterminator**

Now we have to synchronize our watches and adjust our nozzles and get ourselves ready.

**2nd Exterminator**

You'd better get out of here, lady. Without a gas mask you're as good as dead.

> FORENSIC'S VOICE *is heard from under table.*

**Forensic's Voice**
Sing something, Oolan.
**Oolan**
What?
**Emmet**
Anything.

> OOLAN *starts singing "Ahab the Arab" and looking at the audience. The* EXTERMINATORS *turn and cross to* OOLAN. *She keeps singing and smiles at them. They see the table and cross up right and stare at it. They cross back to* OOLAN *and stare at her, then back to the table. This happens several times as* OOLAN *sings:*

## AHAB THE ARAB

Well, let me tell you 'bout Ahab the Arab, the
    sheik of the burning sands,
He had emeralds and rubies just a drippin' offa
    him and a ring on every finger of his hand.
He wore a big old turban wrapped around his
    head and a scimitar by his side,
And every evening about midnight he'd jump on
    his camel named Clyde.

And he'd ride,
Thru the desert night, to the Sultan's tent
Where he would secretly make love to Fatima of
    the seventh veil.
And as he rode, he sang:
Yodli yadli yidli i o,
Nyodli nyadli i o.
Which is Arabic for "Whoa, Clyde."

And Clyde, he say:
Nghee hgraargh norcghhh hargghh
    *(grunting noises)*
Which is camel for "O.K., baby."

Well, he brought his camel to a screeching halt
In the rear of Fatima's tent.

Jumped off Clyde, ducked around the corner,
And into the tent he went.

There he saw Fatima,
Layin' on a zebra skin rug.
With rings on her fingers and bells on her toes,
And a bone in her nose. Ho-ho . . .

BY RAY STEVENS

**1st Exterminator**
ALL RIGHT, STOP THAT SINGING!
> OOLAN *stops and giggles.*
Now what happened to that table, lady?
> OOLAN *turns around and looks at the table.*

**Oolan**
Oh my god!
> *She faints in the arms of the* 2ND EXTERMINATOR, *who catches her.*

**2nd Exterminator**
Great.

**1st Exterminator**
Well, put her down, you dope.
> *He lets* OOLAN *fall to the floor.*

**2nd Exterminator**
We gotta think fast, Forensic, or we're screwed.

**1st Exterminator**
What did you call me? Forensic? Is that what you called me? What kind of a name is that?

**2nd Exterminator**
I don't know. I don't know what came over me.

**1st Exterminator**
Now look. Didn't you and I both see that table over here when we first came in here?

**2nd Exterminator**
Gee, I don't know.

**1st Exterminator**
What do you mean? Wasn't it you that said we could tell we were at the right place on account of the table being where it was, which was right here, not over there. Wasn't

it you who said that to her? Answer me, mushmouth. Was it me or you!

**2nd Exterminator**

It was me, but it still seems like the right place even with the table over there.

**1st Exterminator**

But we can't be sure now. Before, we could be absolutely sure, but now there's some doubt. Am I right? Am I right or wrong!

**2nd Exterminator**

I guess.

**1st Exterminator**

So that means we'll have to call the home office before we can make another move. Am I right? Where's your phone, lady?

**2nd Exterminator**

She's fainted or something.

> EMMET'S VOICE *is heard from under table.*

**Emmet's Voice**

There's a pay phone just down the road.

**1st Exterminator**

There's probably a pay phone just down the road, so why don't you go down there and call while I stay here?

**2nd Exterminator**

Down the road?

**1st Exterminator**

Yeah. Now hurry up! I'm going to be right here waiting. Just ask them if it makes any difference where the table is.

**2nd Exterminator**

O.K. You're going to wait here?

**1st Exterminator**

Yeah. Now move!

> 2ND EXTERMINATOR *exits.* 1ST EXTERMINATOR *looks around, then moves over to* OOLAN, *who is still on the floor. He stares at her, then takes off his helmet and gas mask. He takes off the tank and then kneels down beside* OOLAN *with his back to the table. He stares at* OOLAN's *face for a while,*

*then touches her shoulder. The table suddenly moves down stage, right behind* 1ST EXTERMINATOR. *He kisses* OOLAN *on the forehead, then takes off his gun belt and holster. He lies down beside* OOLAN *and stares at her, then puts his arm around her.* FORENSIC *and* EMMET *come out from under the table very quietly and slowly.* 1ST EXTERMINATOR *kisses* OOLAN *on the lips.* FORENSIC *picks up the tank and gas mask.* EMMET *picks up the gun and holster.* 1ST EX-TERMINATOR *pulls* OOLAN *close to him and hugs her.* EMMET *puts on the gun while* FORENSIC *puts on the tank and gas mask. This all happens while* 1ST EXTERMINATOR *squeezes* OOLAN *and kisses her and strokes her hair.*

Oh my darling. You mustn't worry now. We'll get you out. I'll get you far away to a safe place where we can be quiet and you won't even know. Just relax. All you'll see is smoke filling up the valley. We'll be very high up. Don't you worry about that. It was a tree house but now it's a fort. It's very strong and beautiful. You can trust it to keep you safe and sound. It's colored just like the trees. Orange and yellow and green and blue. And it makes sounds like birds and dogs and wild boar. Really. If anyone comes you can see them from two miles off. You can signal to me if I'm not around. But I always will be. I'll never leave for a second. You can count on me. If you could only see me now I know you'd believe me. If you could wake up in my arms and act like I was sup-posed to be here. Like I always was here and always will be. If you could wake up like that then we could go away from here now. Right this very minute. We could leave and live in the trees.

> EMMET *has the gun on* 1ST EXTERMINATOR. FORENSIC *points the nozzle at him.*

**Emmet**

All right, Big Bopper, on your feet.

> 1ST EXTERMINATOR *jumps to his feet and raises his hands.* OOLAN *gets up.*

**Oolan**

What a nasty rotten trick.

**Forensic**

Shut up!

*FORENSIC crosses to* 1ST EXTERMINATOR, *holding the nozzle on him.*

So you're a lover in disguise. Is that it, Big Bopper? You're really full of pizzazz but you just got led astray. Is that the story?

**1st Exterminator**

Don't press that nozzle!

**Emmet**

Just keep your hands raised up there.

**Oolan**

Don't press that nozzle! We'll all go up in flame!

**Forensic**

It's not a torch. It's gas. Toxic gas. Highly poison toxic gas that when you breathe it you're dead right away.

**1st Exterminator**

Don't be ridiculous.

**Forensic**

WHAT! WHAT DID YOU SAY, SMART ALECK! DON'T GET SMART, MISTER, OR I'LL GAS YOUR ASS!

**Emmet**

Take it easy, Forensic.

**Forensic**

Well, he's a wise guy.

**1st Exterminator**

That gas is for roaches, rats and varmints. Not people. It just gets you sick and makes your eyes water.

**Forensic**

What?

**Emmet**

Wait a minute. Now just take it easy.

**Forensic**

He's trying to come off like a killer of pests and bugs.

**Emmet**

Just don't get excited. We might find out something. Are you hungry, mister?

**1st Exterminator**

No.

**Emmet**
Well, I am. Would you mind if the two of us sat down at the table and I ate some Rice Krispies while I ask you some questions?

**1st Exterminator**
All right.

**Forensic**
What is this?

**Emmet**
Go fetch the Rice Krispies, Oolan.

**Oolan**
You know he has a friend somewhere out there in a phone booth who's going to come back here.

**Emmet**
Just get the Krispies, woman!

**Oolan**
Jesus.

> *She exits.*

**Emmet**
Now set yourself down here, mister. Come on. Just fold your hands on top of your head.

> 1ST EXTERMINATOR *clasps his hands on top of his head and sits in the stage left chair.* EMMET *keeps the gun on him and sits in the stage right chair.*

**Forensic**
Now what am I supposed to do, goddamnit?

**Emmet**
Now then, mister, I take it you've come a long way. Not just from down the block or down the road.

**1st Exterminator**
Well, yes. I mean, that depends.

**Emmet**
I take it you have certain tools at your disposal which provide photographs and details of our layout here. Like table positions, etc.

**1st Exterminator**
That goes without saying. What's the name of that girl?

**Emmet**

I'll give you a hint. It sounds like it might have something to do with tea but it doesn't.

**Forensic**

What the fuck am I supposed to do?

**1st Exterminator**

Darjeeling?

**Emmet**

Now your home office must be getting pretty edgy to send a couple toughs like you, all equipped and everything. Hot and ready. They must suspect a move on our part but the amazement is that we have no idea they had any interest in our project what so ever. I mean you just show up out of the clear blue sky. We don't even have any dogs.

**1st Exterminator**

Dogs?

**Emmet**

Doberman pinschers, German shepherds, wire haired pointing griffons circling the place, sniffing for trouble, ready to tear out a throat on those that smell of a different turf. Do you understand? No young blond dopey muscle boys practicing jujitsu on the front lawn. We're vulnerable as all get out. We've left ourselves with our drawers down. That gives you all the room to plunge in and you have. Which means for us that we temporarily have to abandon the idea of temporarily abandoning the project and throw ourselves once again into the meat of the game. You've forced our hand, as it were.

> 1ST EXTERMINATOR *takes his hands down.* FORENSIC *starts circling the stage restlessly with the gas mask and tank still on.*

**Emmet**

Keep up those hands.

**Forensic**

We don't need this. I'm telling you. We're not going to find out anything more or better by interrogation than we are by going out there and seeing for ourselves what the place looks like. What its potentials are for collapsing. We can't sit around all abstracted out of shape while they lie stacked up on top of each other behind steel doors. It just isn't fair.

**1st Exterminator**

What's her approximate age?

**Emmet**

Thirty-two, twenty-one, thirty.

**1st Exterminator**

Does she see many boys? Young ones? Do they come to her door? Do they sit outside in the driveway honking in their Cobras with their right arm coaxing and kneading and fondling the tuck and roll and their left hand pumping, squeezing on the wheel?

**Emmet**

Do you have a master's degree, mister?

**1st Exterminator**

Not at all.

**Emmet**

What qualifies you then for a job in the line of gasing?

**1st Exterminator**

I'm past my prime.

**Forensic**

So he goes for the skirt, does he? Perhaps we could make a deal.

**Emmet**

Forget it, Forensic. We got her out of there once, or don't you remember? Now you want to start the whole thing over. Put her in a position for being taken back. You don't think clearly. BOMB THE MOTHER FUCKERS! We got her out and she stays out and she ain't going back for no kind of deal. Not even for the most precise, delicate ground plan of the new plumbing system that they just recently put in. Not even for that.

**1st Exterminator**

You mean to say that you'd consider some sort of trade?

Some information for her inspiration. I'll do it, by jove.
I'll do it just as sure as you're standing there.

**Emmet**

Keep those hands up.

> FORENSIC *tears off the gas mask and the tank and lays them on the floor. He goes to the table.*

**Forensic**

Now you're talking.

> EMMET *stands and paces around.* FORENSIC *takes his place in the chair facing* 1ST EXTERMINATOR, *who takes his hands down and slowly begins to stroke himself and grope his own crotch.*

**Emmet**

Out of the question. Absolutely out of the question. We
can't jeopardize her position. It's ridiculous. She'd be
right back in solitary or something worse. She'd be
stacked up right along with the rest of them.

**Forensic**

Big Bopper, you are on the brink of having for your very
own the hottest little discotheque mama ever to come on
the set.

> OOLAN *enters with a bowl, milk and a box of Rice Krispies. She crosses to the table.*

**Emmet**

Oh good. It's about time. Bring it down here.

> *He crosses down right and sits cross legged on the floor.* OOLAN *goes and stands beside him.*

**1st Exterminator**

Oh that's fantastic. I'll tell you anything.

**Forensic**

O.K., first off, do you have a map of the plant?

**1st Exterminator**

Map? Map. Yes I do. Of course I do. But I don't think the
plumbing is included in the detail. I mean. . . .

> *He pulls out a map and hands it across the table to* FO-RENSIC, *then goes on groping himself as he watches* OOLAN.

**Forensic**

Let me see it. Come on, come on.

    FORENSIC *opens the map and spreads it on the table in front of him.*

**Oolan**

Emmet, you'll never in a million years guess what I just a little while ago figured out in the kitchen.

**Emmet**

Come on, come on. Krispies, woman. Gimme Krispies.

**Oolan**

I know, but it's about that. It's about Krispies and the complaint you've had against them all these years. The complaint being that you always lose a few of them because as soon as you add milk to a full bowl they rise up and overflow the bowl and fall on the floor. So what you've had to do all this time is fill the bowl half full, add the milk, mush the half filled bowl down into the milk so they get soggy and don't rise, then add more fresh Krispies on top of those and then a little more milk and then mush the fresh ones down so that the whole bowl is soggy and then finally add the sugar and then finally you get to taste the very first spoonful after having gone through that long painful process.

**Emmet**

Yes, I know, I know. That why I always have good woman fix Krispies so that man not have to go through so much pain.

**Oolan**

I know, but what I'm saying is that I've solved that whole problem.

**Emmet**

Good, good.

**Oolan**

I'll show you how to do it.

**Emmet**

Good.

**Oolan**

O.K., now first I pour the Krispies in. All the way full.

    *She fills the bowl with Rice Krispies.*

Now I put both my hands gently but firmly on top of the Krispies like this.

> SHE *puts her hands on the Krispies and looks at* EMMET.

**Emmet**
Yeah?

**Oolan**
Now you pour the milk.

**Emmet**
Over your hands?

**Oolan**
Yes. Go ahead. Don't be afraid.

**Emmet**
I don't want somebody's grimy hands in my cereal.

**Oolan**
Just pour the milk.

> EMMET *picks up the milk and pours it over* OOLAN's *hands. She smiles at him. He sets down the milk and looks at her. She takes her hands off the cereal.*

See?

> EMMET *picks up a spoon and starts eating ravenously as* FORENSIC *speaks.*

**Forensic**
Listen here, this is no use to us. It's all in some sort of code or something. Everything's mixed up, according to this. Hey, what are you doing? Hey! Hands above the table, mister. HANDS ABOVE THE TABLE!

> 1ST EXTERMINATOR *quickly puts his hands on the table and faces* FORENSIC.

Look, you're going to have to earn this woman, mister. This map doesn't show anything whatsoever where the central stockade is, where the ammunition's kept, where the officers stay, where the guard towers are, where the electric source is, not to mention food and what means of transportation they have in case of a pursuit. None of that's down here. How do you account for that? What's this map for?

**1st Exterminator**
I don't know. They hand it to us. The first day we get

uniforms, helmets, guns, tanks, gas and they hand us that map. One apiece. We each get one to study when we go home. We each are told to memorize the details of this map and to make sure we have them by the next morning because we are going to be thoroughly tested and re-tested on these details. But we never are. Each morning we're never tested and each evening we're threatened that we will be tested the next morning. But we never are.

*He puts his hands down and starts groping again.*

**Forensic**
Ah ha! I get the picture.

*He picks up the map, stands, walks around the table to 1ST EXTERMINATOR and begins interrogating him. OOLAN just watches EMMET as he devours the Rice Krispies. Each time he finishes a bowlful she fills the bowl again and he goes on eating.*

Let's just see what kind of homework you claim you've been doing then. You wouldn't mind that, I'm sure. After all, you've studied so hard night after night and each morning you've been disappointed. So it's about time you had a chance to show your stuff. Don't you think?

**1st Exterminator**
Does she care about things like popularity and letter-men's jackets?

**Forensic**
Now pay attention, swabbie!

*1ST EXTERMINATOR snaps to attention in his seat. He salutes and puts his hands on the table. FORENSIC circles him with the map in his hands.*

**Emmet**
Good. Krispies. Good.

**Forensic**
What's the capital of the state of Arizona!

**1st Exterminator**
Phoenix.

**Forensic**
How much barbed wire does it take to encircle four hundred acres!

**1st Exterminator**
Nine thousand two hundred and seventy square yards.
**Forensic**
How many guns on the east wall facing the western barricade?
**1st Exterminator**
Forty-five.
**Forensic**
On which side are the women kept!
**1st Exterminator**
South west corner and north east.
**Forensic**
Two parts? The women are split in two parts?
**1st Exterminator**
Yes, sir.
**Forensic**
Which two again? Again! Which two!
**1st Exterminator**
North east and south west.
**Forensic**
And the men!
**1st Exterminator**
North west and south east.
**Forensic**
And the dogs!
**1st Exterminator**
Right in the middle and all around the edges.
**Forensic**
Which edges! Make yourself clear, Forensic. Which edges!
**1st Exterminator**
Every edge. All the way around.
**Forensic**
On the sides then. All around the sides. Wouldn't that be a better way to put it?
**1st Exterminator**
Yes.

**Forensic**
And are they chained, tied, on leashes attached to men, running wild, vicious, kind, what kind of dogs?

**1st Exterminator**
Dobermans, shepherds. Griffons.

**Forensic**
Where's the light source now? Where does it come from? How much wattage? What kind of lamps?

**1st Exterminator**
Three million kilowatts, underground, double spots, ninety inch strobes. . . .

**Forensic**
Wait a minute. Underground? Underground! What's underground?

**1st Exterminator**
Light source, sir.

**Forensic**
Underground light source. How? What kind? How is that possible?

**1st Exterminator**
Underground streams, sir.

**Forensic**
Water?

**1st Exterminator**
Yes, sir. That's right, sir. Water.

**Forensic**
I'll be damned. How deep?

**1st Exterminator**
What?

**Forensic**
How deep down! The water! How many feet?

**1st Exterminator**
Oh. I can't reveal that kind of information, sir. That's not part of the test.

**Forensic**
Ah ha!

> *He grabs the pen off the table and marks a big check on the map, then sets down the pen.*

Not part of the test indeed! You were doing so well for so long.

**1st Exterminator**

What do you mean? That's not part of the test, how deep.

**Forensic**

All right, all right. We'll go on. Now then, how many guards are standing on the right wall facing the embankment overlooking the pond?

**1st Exterminator**

Wait a minute. I know how deep it is but I'm not supposed to tell.

**Forensic**

Never mind. How many guards?

**1st Exterminator**

Don't you want to know how deep?

**Forensic**

How many guards!

> EMMET *gorges himself faster and faster as the interrogation gets more intense.* OOLAN *keeps filling the bowl.* FORENSIC *paces around the table.*

**1st Exterminator**

Sixty feet deep!

**Forensic**

AH HA! What kind of pumps! Hydraulic, electric, gas! What kind of pumps!

**1st Exterminator**

Vacuum, sir.

**Forensic**

They run on air then. DO THEY RUN ON AIR!

**1st Exterminator**

Yes, sir.

**Forensic**

AND IF THE AIR WERE TO BE CUT OFF WHERE WOULD IT BE CUT OFF AT!

**1st Exterminator**

At the throttle, sir.

**Forensic**

AT THE THROTTLE! WHAT DOES THAT MEAN, AT THE

THROTTLE? DON'T YOU MEAN AT THE THROAT? CUT
IT OFF AT THE THROAT! DON'T YOU MEAN THAT?
ANSWER YES OR NO!

**1st Exterminator**
Yes.

**Forensic**
THEN HOW DO WE GET TO THE THROAT, FORENSIC!

**1st Exterminator**
Through the back, sir.

> *Loud banging again as before.* EMMET *jumps to his feet with
> the package of Rice Krispies clutched to his chest.* 1ST
> EXTERMINATOR *jumps up and grabs* OOLAN, *holding her
> tightly as though a bomb is about to drop.* EMMET *and* FO-
> RENSIC *rush around the stage not knowing what to do.*

**Emmet**
Hide the Krispies! Hide the Krispies! What'll we do?

**Forensic**
Under the table, Emmet!

**Emmet**
Oolan!

**1st Exterminator**
Leave her alone!

**Forensic**
Under the table, Oolan!

**Emmet**
Take the Krispies! Take the Krispies!

> OOLAN *grabs the Krispies from* EMMET *and hides under the
> table.* 1ST EXTERMINATOR *follows her. Another loud knock.*

**Forensic**
Not him! Just her! Just Oolan!

**1st Exterminator**
Leave her alone!

**Emmet**
Yes! Who is it, please!

> 2ND EXTERMINATOR'S VOICE *over a microphone.*

**2nd Exterminator**
IT'S THE EXTERMINATOR, LADY!

**Emmet**
I'm no lady, mister! I'm a man!
**Forensic**
Don't talk like a dumb kid, Forensic. Open the door.
**Emmet**
Fuck you. This is my home. Give me that gun.
**Forensic**
Stand back, Emmet, or I'll blow you wide open.
> EMMET *lunges at* FORENSIC *and grabs the gun. They struggle with the gun. Another loud knock.*

**2nd Exterminator's Voice**
OPEN THIS DOOR OR I'LL BREAK IT DOWN!
> EMMET *and* FORENSIC *struggle all over the stage with the gun. Long loud ripping sound of door being crashed in. At the end of the sound,* 2ND EXTERMINATOR *falls onto the stage. He is still dressed in the uniform but without gas mask and tank. A pause as* EMMET *and* FORENSIC *look at the* 2ND EXTERMINATOR. *They both have hold of the gun and neither of them lets go until the end of the play. The* 2ND EXTERMINATOR *gets up slowly and brushes himself off. He looks around the stage.*

**2nd Exterminator**
Boy, is it ever weird out there. Have you guys ever been out there?
**Forensic**
Out where?
**2nd Exterminator**
Out there. You haven't got much time, though. I should tell you that right away. Fair warning and all that sort of stuff. Now what's happened to Forensic?
> *He starts looking around as* EMMET *and* FORENSIC *tug at the gun.*

**Emmet**
What's weird out there, mister? I've been out there before and there hasn't been anything weird. What's so weird?
**2nd Exterminator**
The whole thing. The road and everything. The phone booth. The road. Do you suppose he left or something? I suppose so. It's better, I guess.

**Forensic**

What's better? What's weird about the road? Make yourself clear!

**2nd Exterminator**

Especially the road. Just walking along in a gas mask and looking the way I look and everything. I mean there's not many people, but if you run across anybody while you're out there it's really weird. But you'd better get out before it's too late. They'll be here before you can say Jack Robinson.

**Emmet**

Who?

**2nd Exterminator**

I suppose what he did was he just decided to quit the whole business. I suppose that's it. He just got tired of waiting around. Left his gear and everything. In fact we must have decided the very same thing at the very same time but we just happened to be in different places is all. That's it, I'll bet. I'll bet that's what happened. Just as I put down the receiver and folded the glass door open and stepped outside and looked down at the tank and the mask leaning up against the tree trunk and a semi roaring by, just as he, standing around this table, hears the same semi roaring by and takes off the mask and sets down the tank, just as I leave the tank and the mask leaning up against the tree trunk and start following the semi down the road, just as he leaves the room with the tank and the mask sitting here on the floor and starts walking toward— We must have passed each other somewhere. That's it. I'll bet that's what happened. He starts walking toward the phone booth and I start back toward the house and we missed each other on the road. I'll bet you that's the way it happened. But you guys had better get out. They're going to gas this place once and for all.

> *Very slowly blue smoke starts drifting onto the stage. It keeps up until the stage is completely covered and all you can hear are the voices of the actors. It gradually pours over*

*into the audience and fills up the entire theatre by the end of the play. It could change colors in the course of filling the place up, from blue to pink to yellow to green.*

**Forensic**

Who is? You're out of your mind! Gimme the gun, Emmet.

**Emmet**

He's lying, Forensic. Can't you see that? He's not in any hurry to get out, so why should we be?

**2nd Exterminator**

I suppose if I just wait around he's bound to turn up. Fat chance of finding him this time of night, walking along in the dark. Barely see your own nose in front of your own face. Nice place you boys have.

*He sits in the stage left chair, puts his feet on the table and leans back with his hands folded behind his head. EMMET and FORENSIC tug at the gun.*

**Forensic**

He's not either lying. He's called the home office and found out where the table's supposed to be and they're sending men out to help him. He's waiting around for his men. Now gimme the gun, Emmet.

**Emmet**

He just told you that he left all his gear back at the phone booth and he came back to meet his buddy. They're deserters, Forensic!

**2nd Exterminator**

Yep. A place like this could get a man dreaming about settling down. Finding some roots. A kind of headquarters. A place to come back to.

**Forensic**

This is our home!

**2nd Exterminator**

Where's that woman, Emmet?

**Emmet**

What?

**2nd Exterminator**

That woman you had here before.

*OOLAN giggles under the table; nobody hears.*

**Emmet**
Oh she. . . .
**Forensic**
Don't tell! Don't you tell him anything!
**2nd Exterminator**
The trouble is, what if he arrived at the phone booth, found my tank and mask leaning up against the tree trunk and thought the same thing as me at the very same time but in two different places? What if he's set himself down inside the phone booth or up against the tree and he's waiting for me thinking the same thing as me; that it's too damn dark to go walking back on that road at this time of night. What if that's the way it is?
**Emmet**
Then you'd better walk back and get him.
**2nd Exterminator**
No, no. You don't understand. If either one of us makes another move like the moves we've already made then the whole thing could go on forever. Now is a very crucial time. We have to each think individually what the other one is going to do or we'll just miss each other again and again and we'll finally give up and go our separate ways. Do you get what I mean?
**Forensic**
Maybe he doesn't even want to meet you, though. Did you ever think of that?
**Emmet**
Shut up!
**2nd Exterminator**
Maybe you're right, Forensic. Maybe you're absolutely right. Maybe he doesn't. That means he could be somewhere altogether different from the phone booth. That means he could be anywhere.
**Forensic**
That means he could be right under the table even.
**Emmet**
Will you shut up!

**2nd Exterminator**
He most certainly could be, Forensic. He most certainly could. Right under my very nose. Right under the table. But that means I'm right then. That both of us are thinking the very same thing at the very same time. But if he's under the table then we're also in the very same place. I hardly think that could be true, Forensic, because if it were then it could mean only one thing. That he not only doesn't want to meet *me* but he also doesn't want *me* to meet *him*.

> 1ST EXTERMINATOR'S VOICE *is heard from under table.*

**1st Exterminator's Voice**
Now you got the picture.

> OOLAN *giggles.* EMMET *and* FORENSIC *tug at the gun.*

> 2ND EXTERMINATOR *stands and paces around the table. He addresses the table.*

**2nd Exterminator**
Then I take it the whole thing's off. Do I take it right? Do I take it right or wrong?

**1st Exterminator's Voice**
Right! You take it absolutely right.

**2nd Exterminator**
Then we just split up and go our different ways.

**1st Exterminator's Voice**
That's up to you. I'm staying here.

**Emmet**
Will you give me the gun!

**2nd Exterminator**
I called the home office, you know.

**1st Exterminator's Voice**
I know, I know.

**2nd Exterminator**
Then I take it you know what's going to happen.

**1st Exterminator's Voice**
You take it right.

**Forensic**
What's going to happen?

**2nd Exterminator**
And even so you're willing to stay. Even knowing what's going to happen. You're going to stay here.
**1st Exterminator's Voice**
Yes, I am. I've fallen in love.
**Emmet**
What's going to happen?
**2nd Exterminator**
You don't care if we win or lose, then. You don't care if I stay or go. You just don't care. YOU JUST DON'T CARE, FORENSIC!
**Forensic**
Yes, I do! What's going to happen?
**1st Exterminator's Voice**
Why don't you leave? You don't have to stay.
**2nd Exterminator**
Me? Alone? You want me to go running out there alone and go skipping up to them in my fancy new uniform and wave and throw kisses maybe and say hey fellas you've got the wrong house, you've got the wrong farm, you've got the wrong lawn. There's nothing here to exterminate. It's just us. It's just us and a few of our gang. Really. Try the next ranch. Try next door or down the road a piece. Down where they've got all the dogs. Down where you hear all the screaming 'til late in the night. We don't even play the phonograph after eleven o'clock. You can ask them if you like. Just down the road there. They'll tell you. Not a complaint in over thirty-five years. You can come in and look but it's just like I say. It's just a bunch of friends not knowing what else to do. Having breakfast now and then. It's pretty dirty but come right on in. Sure, search wherever you like. You won't find a thing. What do you think we are? Patsys or something? What do you think? Sure, tear up the bed, tear off the sheets, rip out the drawers, tear off our clothes. You won't find a thing. Guns? Guns? You think we have guns? Not on your life. Where would we hide guns? Under the floor? Under the

floor! You hit the nail right on the old head. Guns under the floor. Under the table. Guns all over the place. See for yourselves. Every turn you make there's another gun. Automatics, elephant guns, Marlin four hundreds. Knock yourselves out. Well, I'm not going to do that, Forensic. I'm not going out there ever again. I'm staying right here!

*Loud banging is heard as before. The smoke by this time has filled up the stage and poured over into the audience. The banging keeps up at short intervals and develops a kind of mounting rhythm. This lasts for quite a while as the smoke gradually begins to thin out. Finally, as the smoke disappears, the actors, tables and chairs are all gone so that the audience is looking at empty space at the end.*

## THE END

# The Holy Ghostly

THE HOLY GHOSTLY was first produced by the New Troupe under the direction of Tom O'Horgan on the 1969 European and American college tour.

## Scene:

*The desert at night. A large campfire glows in the center, the audience sits around it in a circle. POP, in his late fifties, is sleeping face up with a hat over his face in a sleeping bag. ICE, his son, in his twenties, is squatting by the fire roasting marshmallows. He wears a hat, blue jeans, boots, vest and a blanket thrown over his shoulders. Around the fire are various cooking utensils, packs and empty cans. It looks as though they've been living there for a while. Blue light fades up slowly.*

**Ice**

    *Singing softly.*

Oh didn't he ramble. Rambled all around.
Rambled 'round the town. Oh didn't he ramble.
  Rambled all around.
Rambled 'round the town. Oh didn't he ramble.
  Rambled all around.
Rambled 'round the town. Oh boy didn't he ever
  ramble. Rambled

'round the town. Rambled all around. That boy
sure did ramble.
Rambled all around. Lookin' at the ground. Oh
didn't he ramble
Rambled all around. Rambled 'round the town. Oh
didn't he ramble.
Rambled all around. All around the town.

*He takes the marshmallow out of the fire and tests it with
his tongue, then sticks it back in the fire.*

Oh didn't he ramble. Rambled all around. All
around the town.
Oh didn't he ramble. Rambled all around. All
around the town.

*POP sits up fast, pulling a gun out from under his pillow and
aiming it at ICE, who sits there coolly.*

I've been trying to get that particular toasty golden brown
that you like, Pop, but it sure takes a long time. So much
easier just to stick it directly in the flames and let her
burn.

**Pop**
What do ya' think I am, a cannibal or somethin'. I like
'em cooked proper or not at all.

**Ice**
Well, you just lay back there and take a load off and I'll
let you know.

**Pop**
You seen the Chindi?

**Ice**
Now if I had, do you think I'd be sitting here toasting
marshmallows and worrying whether or not they're getting too brown or too black?

**Pop**
Just don't go gettin' confident on me. He's a sneaky devil.
**Ice**
Go to sleep.

**Pop**

I have an idea you probably think yer old man's teched in the head. You probably do.

**Ice**

Go to sleep.

**Pop**

You do, don't ya'? Don't ya'?

**Ice**

If I did, do you really think I'd have dropped everything I had going for myself in New York City, grabbed the nearest Greyhound bus and wound up out here in the Badlands with you?

**Pop**

All what you had going in New York City? All what? My ass. You were just another bug in the rug, boy. Gimme that marshmallow and stop playin' with it.

> POP *reaches over and grabs the marshmallow off the end of the stick. He pops it in his mouth.* ICE *takes another one out of a bag and puts it on the stick.*

Now listen to me. I could care less whether or not you believe in ghosts and phantoms. The reason I asked ya' out here weren't for sympathy and it sure as hell weren't for yer instincts. Lord knows those a' been shot to shit in that damn city. I plain and simple need an extra gun.

**Ice**

Then why didn't you hire one?

**Pop**

Not to be trusted! None of 'em. Get an old man like me out here in the desert alone and right away they'd take me for everything I got.

**Ice**

Which is exactly what? Let me see. A fishing knife, a John B. Stetson circa 1890, a Colt 45, a Browning over and under. . . .

**Pop**

Yer so smart! Yer so goddamn smart! Look at ya'! Just look at ya'!

**Ice**

Spittin' image of his old man. Yessir. Why if it weren't for the age separatin' 'em you'd think they was the same person.

**Pop**

Yer no son a' mine. No son a' mine woulda' gone and changed his name and dressed his self up like a hillbilly.

**Ice**

Well, I didn't know we were in a fashion show.

**Pop**

Yer so goddamn smart, aren't ya'.

**Ice**

Well, I had me some good teachers. Sheep ranchers and horse thieves and what all. Taught me everything I know.

**Pop**

I'm tellin' you, boy, you don't know what fear's all about. You ain't even begun to taste it.

**Ice**

How's the marshmallow?

**Pop**

Fair to middlin'.

**Ice**

They say men make better cooks than women.

**Pop**

Do they now.

**Ice**

Why don't you stop coming on like a hard on? I'm the only company you've got.

**Pop**

That's what you think. That's really what you think, ain't it? What if I was to tell you there was a Chindi out there with more faces and more arms and legs than the two of us put together? You really think we're alone, don't ya', boy? You think we're just a sittin' out here in the starry night passin' the time a day and roastin' marshmallows like a couple a Boy Scouts away from their mothers.

**Ice**
You told me he looked just like you.

**Pop**
Who?

**Ice**
The Chindi.

**Pop**
Sometimes he does. Sometimes he does that just to trick me. Trick me into believin' it's all a figment a' my imagination. But I know better. I know he's out there waitin'. Waitin' for me to make a wrong move. Bidin' his time. Smellin' my campfires. Pushin' his toe into the holes my body made when it was asleep.

**Ice**
Listen, I got an idea. You say he's out there waiting for us and we're here waiting for him. Right?

**Pop**
That's about the size of it.

**Ice**
Then why don't we push him? Lean on him a little. Ghosts don't count on that. They count on fear. We might scare the shit out of him if we went after his ass.

**Pop**
And how do you figure on trackin' him, smart boy? Ever seen a ghost make tracks?

**Ice**
We could pretend we were leaving. He'd come after us and then we'd get him. If we split up, one of us behind, me behind and you in front. We'd get him in the middle.

**Pop**
Go to sleep.

**Ice**

Look, Pop, I gotta get back to the city. All my friends are there. I can't be diddling around here in the desert forever.

**Pop**

Important business. Big man. Big important man. Go ahead then! Go on! Go off and leave yer old Dad. Go ahead!

> *He rolls back into the sleeping bag and puts the hat back over his face.*

**Ice**

Will the radio bother you? Pop?

> *No answer from* POP. ICE *takes a transistor out of his bedroll and turns it on softly to a rock station.*

**Pop**

I'm not in show business, ya' know. There's some people likes to sleep at night. I need my rest. Ice? I said this ain't goddamn New York City where ya' can be playin' the radio at all hours of the goddamn day. Ice!

> *A shrieking, screeching howl is heard. They both jump to their feet with their guns out. Silence. Except for the radio.*

He's there.

**Ice**

Come on. Now's our chance.

> ICE *goes running off.* POP *stays frozen.*

**Pop**

Ice! Ice! Come back here, boy! Come back here! Ice!

> POP *goes to the radio and shuts it off. He turns in a tight circle with his gun out looking into the night.*

I ain't afraid to die. I just want ya' to know that much. I ain't afraid. I had my day.

> *The sound of bells jingling on someone's ankles as he walks.* POP *starts in the direction of the sound.*

I hear ya'. Now look. I don't rightly know what this is all about. I really don't. I figure that somewhere in yer mind you got this idea that I done somethin' to deserve yer comin' after me and torturin' me and maybe killin' me or somethin', but—

*The voice of the* CHINDI *is heard in the dark. He moves onto the stage slowly. A tall figure dressed in black blankets with bells around his ankles, eagle feathers around the wrists and neck and coming out of his head. The face is all white, the rest of the body jet black.*

**Chindi**

You're already dead, Mr. Moss.

**Pop**

How do you know my name?

*The* CHINDI *darts across the stage behind* POP. POP *wheels around and fires. The* CHINDI *sways from side to side and clacks his teeth.*

**Chindi**

Did you change it?

**Pop**

No, I didn't change it. *I* got some pride in tradition. That's my son yer thinkin' of. Ice. He changed his name to Ice. What do ya' think of that? From Stanley Hewitt Moss the seventh to Ice. What do ya' think a' that? It's him yer thinkin' of. Maybe it's him yer after? Is it him yer after?

**Chindi**

I'm not after nobody, Mr. Moss.

*The* CHINDI *darts again to another part of the stage.* POP *wheels and fires twice. The* CHINDI *shakes his feet and slaps his hands on his thighs.*

**Pop**

I done nothin' to deserve this. What've I done! I got a right to live out the rest a' my life in peace. Lord knows I've had a struggle.

**Chindi**

The Lord knows nothin', Stanley.

*The* CHINDI *darts again.* POP *fires. The* CHINDI *smacks his lips.*

**Pop**

Don't go givin' me none a' yer high falootin' esoteric gobbledy gook, Buster Brown. Just 'cause ya' struck off fer the big city on yer own and made a big splash when ya' was just a whipper snapper don't mean ya' can humiliate an old man.

**Chindi**

Why don't you face up to it, Mr. Moss. You're dead.

**Pop**

Get away from me! Stand back! Stand back or I'll blow ya' to kingdom come!

**Chindi**

Come with me, Stanley.

> *The* CHINDI *reaches out his hand for* POP. POP *fires. The* CHINDI *darts to another part of the stage and blows on the back of his hand.*

**Pop**

I don't know what you think you're trying to prove, Ice, but I ain't fallin' for it. Cheap theatrics. That's all! That get-up don't fool yer old Dad for a minute. I suppose ya' thought I'd drop over dead out a' sheer fright. I suppose ya' thought that. You'd like that, wouldn't ya'! Wouldn't ya'! Then with yer old man out a' the way you could step right in and take over the ranch, lock, stock and barrel. All six hundred acres and the sheep to boot. Well, I ain't fallin' for it! Ya' hear me! You hear me, boy!

**Chindi**

You're a fool, Mr. Moss.

> *The* CHINDI *darts off stage and leaves* POP *standing there.*

**Pop**

Now you come back here! Ice! Come back here, ya' damn ingrate! This here has gone further than far enough! I'm yer Pa! There's no reason we can't see this thing out eye to eye! All right! All right, you asked for it. There ain't been any feudin' in the family since 1884 but if that's the way you want it that's the way you'll get it.

> POP *goes to the sleeping bag and pulls it away. Underneath is a bazooka. He hoists it up on his shoulder and takes it over near the campfire. He sets it down and goes back to the sleeping bag and pulls out some shells. The sound of an Indian drum steadily beating is heard off stage.* POP *looks out.*

Ice?

> *He goes to the bazooka and loads a shell into it. The drum keeps drumming.*

Ice! You damn fool! They won't even be able to tell the difference between you and the sand if this thing goes off. Listen to reason, boy.

> POP *mounts the bazooka up on his shoulder and gets it ready to fire.*

I always liked to think of the two of us as blood brothers. Ya' know what I mean? Not father and son but brothers. I mean ever since you was old enough to learn how to shoot a thirty-thirty. The way we used to go out in the jeep late at night and flash the headlights on them jackrabbits. Blastin' them damn jackrabbits all up against the cactus. Remember that, Ice? Them jackrabbits was as big as puppies. Not enough left to even make a decent stew out of by the time we was through. And that old gun. The way that old Winchester used to kick ya' so hard it'd throw ya' right into the back seat. Yessir. Shadow Mountain that was. Those was rich days, boy. We was close as sticky socks back then.

> *The drum gets closer.*

What do ya' want to throw all that away for, Stanley? I know ya' set out to hurt me. Right from the start I knowed that. Like the way ya' changed yer name and all. That was rotten, Stanley. I give ya' that name 'cause that was my name and my Pappy gave me that name and his Pappy before him. That name was handed down for seven generations, boy. Now ain't no time to throw it away. What's gonna happen when you have yerself a son? What's gonna happen to him with a name like Ice? He'll get laughed right out a' school. How's he gonna play football with a name like that? You gotta think on the future, son.

> *The drum continues to get closer.*

I know ya' probably think I was rough on ya' and the truth is I was. But I tried to show ya' the ropes. Tried to give ya' some breaks too. Me, I never had no real breaks. My old man was a dairy farmer. Started hittin' the bottle and lost the whole farm. Things started goin' down hill from that point on. Next thing he got himself a job sellin'

Hershey bars door to door. Never saw much a' Pa then.
Travelin' all around. Chicago, Detroit, Des Moines, Tucumcari, Boise. Then we found out that Pa got his self
so drunk in a hotel room that he fell asleep with a cigar
burning in his hand. Burned the whole hotel right to the
ground with him in it. So I had to go to work. Support the
whole family.

    *The drum continues through the speech.*

Then my brother Jaimie comes home one day complainin'
of a bad pain. Take him to the doctor and come to find
out he's got himself a case a' polio and they're gonna have
to take his leg off. The whole damn leg from the hip down.
That was right around the time a' the great Depression.
'Course you don't remember them days. So me, I'm
workin' night and day in Macy's downtown Chicago and
bringin' home the bacon once a week so Ma can buy the
groceries. By the time Jaimie gets old enough to work
I'm startin' to think on marrying yer mother. 'Course
Jaimie was a cripple but strong as an ox from the waist
up. That come from hoistin' himself up and down stairs
since he was just a squirt. So right away Jaimie goes out
and decides he wants to become a truck driver. Yessir.
That old boy had some real spunk. Walks right up to
Bekins Van and Storage and asks 'em fer a job. Well, they
could see right off that he only had but one good leg and
the other one wood but he figured he was just as good as
the next man. So they sent him to a special school where
he learned how to use that wooden leg a' his. First thing
ya' know he's out there in the real world drivin' a goddamn
Bekins truck with a wooden leg. So me, I get myself
hitched to yer mother and get all set to take off fer college
and get myself a diploma so's I could make me a heap a'
money, when lo and behold if old Uncle Sam don't decide
it's come my time to serve my country. So off I goes to
learn how to fly B-24's and B-17's and drop bombs and
whatall. Italy, Holland, Germany, England, the whole she-
bang. Then I come back with nothin' to show for it but

some Jap rifles and Kraut helmets and little red bombs cut on my leather jacket with a Gillette Blue Blade. Each one showing mission accomplished. Each one showin' I got back alive. But I was feelin' all right 'cause about that time I got myself something to look forward to stateside. I'm comin' home to my little woman in Rapid City, South Dakota, and she's got one hell of a package waiting fer me. She's got me a son. A son with my name and my eyes and my nose and my mouth. My own flesh and blood, boy. My son, Stanley Hewitt Moss the seventh.

> ICE *appears. He has white war paint stripes on his face and an Indian drum in his hand which he beats in a slow steady rhythm.*

**Ice**

Hi, Pop.

**Pop**

Don't call me none a' yer family names.

> ICE *stops beating the drum.*

**Ice**

I saw the Chindi, Pop.

**Pop**

I'll bet you did. I'll bet you could tell me exactly what he looks like too. What he has for breakfast and which side of his crotch he hangs his dick on.

**Ice**

When are you going to stop talking like a dirt farmer? You're an intelligent, mature adult with a lot of potential. Stop putting yourself down.

**Pop**

Ya' see this here?

**Ice**

The bazooka?

**Pop**

It ain't no bazooka. It's a rifle grenade. Made it myself.

**Ice**

Nice work.

**Pop**

Thanks. I was gonna blow yer damn head off fer pullin' that stunt on me, but now I figure it's all fer the best. Ya' helped bolster my courage for when the real thing comes.

**Ice**

You know what he told me? He told me that you were dead and you don't even know it.

*He sits and plays the drum softly with his hands.*

**Pop**

Now we've carried this damn fiasco far enough, boy! I don't know what kind a' fool plan you've got in yer head but if yer tryin' to scare me yer gonna have to go. . . .

**Ice**

Go fuck yourself, you old prick! I'm going back to New York and you can stay here and jerk yourself off forever on this desert!

*ICE starts to leave. POP jumps up and grabs ICE around the shoulders. POP drops his accent.*

**Pop**

All right. All right, Stanley, look. . . .

**Ice**

My name's Ice.

**Pop**

All right. O.K., Ice. Look, we don't have to fight. We really don't. We can be calm and sensible. But all these games you've been. . . .

**Ice**

What games? You call me up person-to-person collect and I can barely understand you because you're so hysterical, and you tell me there's a ghost after your ass and I believe you although it seems a bit far fetched and I drop everything and come whaling out here to meet you and pull you together and now. . . .

**Pop**

I was kidding, though. Just kidding around. I mean. . . .

**Ice**

Kidding? You jive mother fucker! I should blow your head off right here and now.

**Pop**

Wait a minute, Stanley!

**Ice**

GODDAMNIT! You make that mistake again and I'll cut you in half!

**Pop**

I'm sorry! I'm sorry! I just haven't gotten used to it. The sound of it. It doesn't make any sense to me. I'm an old man, son. I'm not used to. . . .

**Ice**

Well, get used to it! Get used to another thing too while you're at it. For eighteen years I was your slave. I worked for you hand and foot. Shearing the sheep, irrigating the trees, listening to your bullshit about "improve your mind, you'll never get ahead, learn how to lose, hard work and guts and never say die" and now I suppose you want me to bring you back to life. You pathetic creep. Hire yourself a professional mourner, Jim. I'm splitting.

**Pop**

No! No, Stanley!

**Ice**

That's it! That's it. I told you. One more time, old man.

> ICE *starts stalking* POP.

**Pop**

Now wait a minute, son.

**Ice**

I'm no son a' yours. Remember? You better go for yer gun, boy. I'm gonna kill you once and fer all. The difference this time is that you'll know that you're dead.

**Pop**

Ice! Don't be a fool! I always taught you never to play around with a weapon. You have to have respect for a gun!

**Ice**
Draw, old timer.

**Pop**
Ice! Have you lost your good sense! I'm your father! Your own flesh and blood!

**Ice**
Abandon the creeping meatball!

**Pop**
You can't turn against your own kind! We're civilized human beings! Just because we don't see things eye to eye on certain political opinions.

**Ice**
Pop, the oppressor's cherry!

**Pop**
I always saw to it that you had a hot meal on the table and a roof over your head. It's just that I'm lonely, Ice. I missed you. Ever since your mother passed on, I've had the most terrible nightmares. Visions of demons and goblins chasing me and taunting me.

**Ice**
Poor baby. Does him do-do-do and pee-pee in his um's bed too?

**Pop**
And you know about my stomach. Ever since the war. I keep seeing slanty eyed faces of faces I never saw. Any minute it could burst and eat into the intestines and then I could die.

**Ice**
You're already dead, dope. You're a ghost.

**Pop**
Be kind, Ice. It's not asking much.

**Ice**
It's asking too much. It's asking the world, Bozo, and I ain't got it to give.

**Pop**
Let's just be friends. Let bygones be bygones, son. Why can't we be friends?

*A white* WITCH *appears with* POP's *corpse on her back, carrying it piggy-back style. The corpse is dressed exactly the same as* POP, *and has a chalk white face. The* WITCH *is dressed in white robes with black feathers on her wrists and neck and coming out of her head. Her face is painted black, with long black hair. She sets the corpse down near the fire facing the flames and warms herself by the flames. The corpse is in a squatting position.*

**Witch**

Lovely evening.

**Ice**

Yeah. Howdy.

**Pop**

Who are you?

**Witch**

I'm the Chindi's old lady. And you're Bozo the Clown.

> *She cackles and laughs like the Witch in* The Wizard of Oz.

**Pop**

What's that thing? It's disgusting. It gives off a stench.

**Witch**

That's your body, Bozo.

**Pop**

Stop calling me that! My name's Stanley Hewitt Moss the sixth.

**Witch**

Far out.

**Pop**

Would you kindly warm yourself up and then remove that stinking mound of flesh and be on your way?

**Witch**

Didn't you tell him, Ice?

**Ice**

I didn't get a chance to. We started arguing.

**Witch**

That's a drag.

**Pop**

What in God's name is going on here? Do you two know each other?

**Ice**

More or less.

**Witch**

Your son's a ballin' fool, Mr. Moss.

**Pop**

Is this another part of your scheme to scare me into admitting I lied to you, Ice? I already admitted that. What more do you want?

**Ice**

To admit that you're dead.

**Pop**

But I'm not dead! I can see! I can touch! I can smell! I can feel! I'm alive!

**Witch**

The Chindi is coming back for you, Mr. Moss.

**Pop**

Well, that's nice. And what am I supposed to do when he comes?

**Witch**

You're to go with him. He'll take you away.

**Pop**

And what if I don't want to go?

**Ice**

You got no choice, Pop. Finally you've got no choice.

**Witch**

You're a ghost, Mr. Moss. Do you know what a ghost is?

**Pop**

I don't know and I don't care. I've never been inclined toward hokus pokus and I'll be damned if I'll start now.

**Witch**

A ghost is one who has died without finishing what he had to do on the earth. Sometimes because they were cut short, like baby ghosts. Sometimes because they never found out what they were here for, like you, Mr. Moss. A ghost is hung up between being dead and being alive because he doesn't know where he's at. We're here to show you exactly where you're at.

**Pop**
You presumptuous little cunt. I have a good mind to take you over my knee and spank you.
**Witch**
Try it.
**Pop**
I'm not a man of violence. I never have been.
**Ice**
Never?
**Pop**
Well, not when I could help it. I was only doing my job. You can't hold that against me.
**Witch**
The Chindi asked me to tell you that you have a certain amount of time between now and when you're going to have to reckon with him. That time is going to be measured by this body, Mr. Moss. Your own body. Which you left and abandoned and tried to get back inside of. By the time rigor mortis completely sets into the body, by the time the body stiffens out straight as a board, the Chindi will be back to take you with him.
**Pop**
And where are we supposedly going?
**Witch**
To a place you'll never come back from.
**Ice**
Never?
**Witch**
Not this time. He had his chance.
**Ice**
Looks like curtains, Pop.
**Witch**
It's better this way, Mr. Moss. Imagine hanging around for eternity in the state of mind you're in now. Strung out between right and wrong, good and evil, the right and the left, the high and the low, the hot and the cold, the old and the young, the weak and the strong, the body and the

spirit. You're a fucking mess. We're going to put you back together again. A whole man. One whole thing. How about it? You'll never be the same again.

**Pop**

> *He goes back into accent.*

No soap, Snow White. And you can tell your Chindi friend that he'd better bring a six shooter if he's aimin' to bring in Stanley Hewitt Moss the sixth!

**Witch**

Well, thanks for the fire, Ice.

**Ice** ʻ

Bye.

> *The white* WITCH *disappears in the night.* POP *is back into his dirt farmer image.*

**Pop**

Well, least we know where we stand now, boy. Least we know who the enemy is. Better dig yerself in there, boy. They'll be a' comin' before long.

> POP *goes back to the bazooka and lies down behind it, mounting it on his shoulder and trying to dig in like a marine, using the pack and sleeping bags as a foxhole.* ICE *sits by the fire and starts beating on the drum. He stares into the eyes of the corpse. The corpse, from this point on, almost imperceptibly stiffens from a sitting position to lying straight out on the ground on his back. Something like a slow motion self-immolation.*

Thing I couldn't get straight was whether or not it was real or not. Know what I mean, boy? Like whether I was just scarin' myself fer no good reason. Hallucinatin' and what not. Well, now we know, I guess. Don't we? I mean now we know it's real. The ghost. Stop playin' that damn fool drum and talk to yer Pa!

> ICE *keeps playing the drum. When he talks to* POP *he directs his speech to the corpse.*

**Ice**

> *His voice changes to a little boy's.*

You're the one who taught me, Daddy. You said practice, practice, practice. That's the only way to do the best.

**Pop**

Well, that's right. It stands to reason. Just look at Gene Krupa, Buddy Rich—how do you think they got where they are today?

**Ice**

Well, look at Sonny Murray, Keith Moon. What about them?

**Pop**

Never heard of 'em. Upstarts. The whole bunch. It takes more than gulldanged imagination to be a great drummer. It takes guts. That's the thing you never learned. You gotta build up yer strength. You gotta work on that left hand so hard you can do a triple paradiddle with yer right hand tied behind yer back. Ya' gotta get yer right foot so strong it's like steel. Work with that ankle so hard that it feels like it's gonna break off. Then when ya' reach that point where ya can hardly stand the pain of it—that's when you start yer real practicin'. That's when yer work begins. Separate all the pieces. Two arms, two hands, two wrists, two legs, two ankles, two feet. Everything in pairs. Break it all down in pairs. Make the pairs work together, with each other. Then make 'em work against each other, independent. Do some cymbal work, just use the ride, then the sizzle, then the splash, then yer high hat. Feel out all the sounds you got at yer disposal, all the tones in a good set a' tubs. Yer high toms, yer lows.

**Ice**

What about cowbells?

**Pop**

Well, if you go fer that Latin hand-drum sound, that's all right too. Congas and bongos and timbalis and Dholaks and Dumbaks. All them catchy calypso, mambo, cha-cha-cha rhythms they got. Helps ya' keep on yer toes. Teaches ya' a lot about what's behind a rhythm structure. Off beats and such. That off beat stuff. Course all the technique in the world ain't gonna mean yer a genius. No sir. Ya' can only go so far with learning the essentials, then the rest is up to you and God.

**Ice**
Were you a genius, Pop?

**Pop**
Me? Naw. Damn good though. One of the two or three fastest in the country. 'Course them were the days of Dixieland and Cajun music. Don't hear much a' that anymore. Mind if I turn the radio on?

**Ice**
I'm not asleep.

**Pop**
I know. But ya' always ask me before you turn it on so I thought I'd extend ya' the same courtesy.

> POP *turns the radio on soft.*

**Ice**
It's just that I know how you hate Rock and Roll.

**Pop**
Now that ain't true, boy. Not a bit. That kinda' music come out a' good roots. Rhythm and blues and country music, Western music. Them's good roots. My gripe was and always has been that it got into the wrong hands. A bunch of teenage morons. That's all. All that "doo,wa, doo,wa, doo,wa, ditty, talk about the girls from New York City." Stuff like that. Like a bunch a' morons. Grates against a man's ears who's played with the best. Why, if I was young today I'd probably be playin' Rock and Roll myself, right along with the rest of 'em. Can't say's I'd go in fer all this transvestite malarkey that's been goin' on though. I'd keep my self respect. But I'd probably figure in the picture somewhere.

**Ice**
You probably would.

**Pop**
Ya' sound far away, boy. What're ya' thinkin'?

**Ice**
Just dreamin' on the fire. You can see the whole world in a fire.

> Pause. POP *sings. During the song he becomes like a little boy.* ICE *becomes like his father.*

**Pop**
> *Sings.*
>
> A beautiful bird in a gilded cage
> A beautiful sight to see
> You may think she's happy and free from fear
> She's not though she seems to be
>
> She flew from the hills at a tender age
> She flew from the family tree
> You may think she got to the promised land
> But she's not where she wants to be.

**Pop**
Ice?

**Ice**
Yeah.

**Pop**
Ice, could you tell me a story? I feel lonely.

**Ice**
Sure. Turn the radio off and come on over here.
> POP *turns off the radio and crawls over to* ICE *and curls up in his lap.* ICE *strokes his forehead and tells him a story. He stops beating the drum. The corpse keeps stiffening through all this.*

**Ice**
Once upon a time millions and millions of years ago, before man was ever around, there was a huge, huge fiery ball of fire.

**Pop**
Like the sun?

**Ice**
Sort of—but much huger and hotter than our sun. A super sun. At the same time, somewhere in space, there was a giant planet made out of cosmic ice.

**Pop**
What's cosmic mean?

**Ice**
Of, or pertaining to, the cosmos.

**Pop**
What's the cosmos?

**Ice**
Everything.

**Pop**
Then what happened?

**Ice**
For millions of years the super sun and the giant ice planet traveled through space, spinning and spinning and spinning. Then one day they collided with each other and the giant ice planet penetrated deep inside to the center of the super sun and buried itself. For hundreds of thousands of years nothing happened until one day suddenly the accumulating steam from the melting ice planet caused an enormous explosion inside the super sun. Fragments of the sun were blown out into outer space. Other fragments fell back on the ice planet. Still other fragments were projected into an intermediate zone.

**Pop**
What's intermediate?

**Ice**
Something in between. These intermediate fragments are what we call the planets in our system. There were thirty fragments which gradually became covered with ice. The moon, Jupiter and Saturn are made out of ice. The canals on Mars are cracks in the ice. The only fragment that wasn't completely ice was the one we're riding on right now. The earth. Ever since then the earth has been carrying on a constant struggle between fire and ice. At the same time as this great explosion, at a distance three times that of Neptune from the earth, there was an enormous band of ice. It's still there and you can see it tonight.

**Pop**
Where?

**Ice**
> *Pointing to the sky.*

Right up there. Astronomers call it the Milky Way because stars shine through it from the other side.

**Pop** ·
It must be really cold up there.
**Ice**
It is.
**Pop**
But we're nice and warm.
**Ice**
Well, we're by the fire.
**Pop**
Won't the ice ever melt though?
**Ice**
Sometimes it does. That's why it rains. Look at the moon.
**Pop**
It seems really close.
**Ice**
It's getting closer all the time. One day it's going to collide with the earth and another battle will go on between fire and ice. It's happened before.
**Pop**
With the moon?
**Ice**
Not this moon but other ones. Three other moons came before this one. And three times the earth was destroyed and made over again.
**Pop**
And it's going to happen again?
**Ice**
Yes.

> POP *jumps up and goes to the bazooka.*

**Pop**
Bull pukey! You really expect me to believe that hokus pokus?

> POP *switches on the radio again.*

**Ice**
No.
**Pop**
The earth ain't no more made out a' ice than the sun is.

Who filled yer brain with that hogwash anyhow? I'll tell ya' who's gonna make and break this planet, boy. We are! You and me and nothing else! We're gonna set this world on fire, boy. Soon's we blow up this Chindi fella and that two-bit whore a' his, we'll be on our way. I'll show ya' a thing or two about fire and ice. I'll show ya' how to make the world spin!

**Ice**

How're you gonna blow him up, Pa?

**Pop**

You'll see. Soon's he sets foot in this camp he's a dead man.

**Ice**

But he's already dead and so are you. You can't kill a dead man.

**Pop**

More hogwash! Fairy tales! What's real is real and there ain't no way around it.

**Ice**

You won't even see him this time. He'll just come for you and take you away and you won't even know he's there.

**Pop**

Why don't you go down by the crick and wash that damn make-up off yer face? If ya' weren't my own son I'd say you was a sissy.

     ICE *stands up.*

**Ice**

I think I will. I think I'll walk to the crick and keep right on walking.

**Pop**

No! Ice! You can't leave me now. There's not much more time. Look at that corpse. It's gettin' stiffer by the minute.

**Ice**

Tell you what. As soon as you blow up the Chindi come straight to Rapid City and we'll meet up there.

**Pop**

No! I need your help!

**Ice**

Really? What for? To load your bazooka?

**Pop**

There must have been some time once when you needed me and I helped you out.

**Ice**

There must have been.

**Pop**

Well, now you can pay me back.

**Ice**

Right.

> *He draws his gun and shoots* POP *in the stomach, then walks off.*

**Pop**

Ice! Ice! Stanley!

> POP *grabs his stomach and staggers around the stage. The corpse is almost completely stiffened out by now.*

Stanley! You can have the ranch! The sheep! The station wagon! The Dodge half ton! The spring tooth harrow! The barbeque pit! The house! You can take it! Take it! I'm not kidding, Stanley! This is no way to leave yer Pa after all these years!

> *To himself.*

The moon's getting closer. I can make out the craters. All of the craters. It's a marvelous thing, Stanley! This is a remarkable time we're living in when a man can look from behind the moon, over his shoulder, past the ice and see that warm, greenish blue planet spinning around and around with its cargo of little people. Don't you think? I agree with you, Stanley! I agree with your philosophy and your political point of view, only don't leave me now! We can argue! That's part of the fun. Ya' can't expect to make an omelette without breaking a few eggs! Conflict's a good thing! It keeps ya on yer toes! Stanley! Yer Pa is dying!

> *Again the screeching howl. The bells of the* CHINDI *are heard as before, getting louder and louder; the corpse is*

*completely stiff.* POP *stops and listens; he runs to the radio and shuts it off.*

So yer really gonna try it after all. Yer really gonna try bringin' in Stanley Hewitt Moss the sixth. Well, come on! Come on then!

*He goes to the bazooka and mounts it on his shoulder. More bells are heard from other parts of the theatre. It should be a live sound, not recorded.*

Come on, ya' weasely little no-count! Sneakin' around in the dark. I can remember the time when wars was fought out in the open field. Hand to hand combat. Teddy Roosevelt style. None a' this sneaky guerrilla stuff that's come into fashion. Hit and run perverts! Throw a grenade and run the other way. Never even see the faces of the dead. Well, I got one shot and I'm gonna make it count. Stanley! That old Chindi thinks he's come to take a patsy off!

POP *pulls his hand away from his stomach and looks at it. It's dripping with blood.*

Wait a minute. Wait a darn minute.

*He crawls over to the fire on his hands and knees. He holds his hand up to the flames so the light shines on it.*

If that don't beat all.

*He rubs his stomach again and holds his hand to the light.*

No blood. A bloodless critter. Not a speck a blood. They was right the whole time. Wait a minute! Stanley! You was right!

*He pulls up his sleeve and slowly, carefully sticks his whole arm into the flames and holds it there.*

No pain. There's no pain!

*He breaks into loud laughter and jumps up. He dances in circles and shouts.*

No pain and no blood! No pain and no blood! No pain and no blood! No pain and no blood!

*He stops for a second and looks into the fire. The sound of the drum starts up again. More bells all over the house in a steady rhythm.*

*In the corpse's face.*

You're a dead man, Stanley. You're a dead man.

*He looks at the corpse.*

A dead body.

> *He walks into the center of the campfire and laughs. He dances in the fire.*

Oh didn't he ramble. Rambled all around. All around the town. Oh didn't he ramble. Rambled all around. All around the town. All around the town. He sure did ramble. Rambled all around. All around the town. Boy, didn't he ramble.

> *He stops and runs out of the fire. He goes to the bazooka and lifts it up, then throws it into the fire. He keeps up the talk as he goes around the stage throwing everything into the fire: sleeping bags, cans, blankets, guns, hats, radio. He leaves the corpse for last. As he throws more and more things into the fire the flames grow higher and spread outside the circle. This could be done with a projector and film loop above the audience. POP is in a maniac state. He talks to the corpse, himself, an imaginary ICE and ghosts he doesn't see.*

Boy, if my boy could see me now! If my boy Stanley was here to see me now! He wouldn't believe it. The change in his old man. A changed man. Believe you me, Stanley, he wouldn't believe it! Imagine me, crawlin' off into the badlands like an old alley cat, knowin' he's dyin', dyin' alone. Tryin' to save pain. Save face. Keep the family calm. No sense in them seeing their man of the house in his last moment on earth. It's a long moment, Stanley! Boy, don't you know if there was a phone booth out here I'd sure make a collect call to that boy and have him hightail it out here to see his old man now! Yessir! That boy would be so proud! He'd fall on his knees to kiss the earth my boots stomp on. It's been a long time. A long, long time. Wonder what he's lookin' like now. A grown man. My boy, a grown man. And his old man, a boy. You're as old as ya feel, Stanley! And I feel as old as forever! I've never been more alive in my life, son! Never been more full a' fire and brimstone. All that useless fear. All them years yelpin' like a pup, afraid to look the eagle in the eyeball. It's never like ya' think it's gonna be, Stanley! Never! Never endless and lonely and no end in sight. Just goin' on and on without a stop. It's right here, boy, in the fire. Ya' take the fire in yer hand, boy, in both hands. And ya' squeeze it to death! Ya squeeze the life out of it. Ya' make it bleed! Ya' whip it and make it dance for ya'. Ya' make it do its dance. Ya' make it scream like a woman with the pain and joy all wrapped up together! Ya' send it beyond fear, beyond death, beyond doubt. There's no end to its possibilities.

*He looks the corpse in the eye.*

*To the corpse.*

And what're you doin'?

**Corpse**

Nothin'.

**Pop**

Don't do nothin' in the kingdom a' God! Burn! Burn! Burn! Burn! Burn! Burn! Burn! Burn!

*He picks up the corpse, holds it over his head and spins it around in circles, then throws it into the fire. The drums and bells increase, the flames flicker all over the audience. The whole theatre is consumed in flames as POP screams over and over and dances in the fire.*

BURN! BURN! BURN! BURN! BURN! BURN! BURN! BURN!

BLACKOUT
THE END

# Back Bog Beast Bait

BACK BOG BEAST BAIT was first produced at the American Place Theatre in April 1971 with the following cast:

| | |
|---|---|
| *Slim* | Beeson Carroll |
| *Shadow* | James Hall |
| *Maria* | Antonia Rey |
| *Preacher* | Bob Glaudini |
| *Gris Gris* | O-Lan Johnson-Shepard |
| *Ghost Girl* | Yolandé Bavan |
| *Beast* | Leroy |

This production was directed by Tony Barsha; lights, Johnny Dodd; set, Richard; costumes, Patty.

**Scene 1:**

The play opens with the song "Back Bog Blues" sung by GHOST GIRL:

## BACK BOG BLUES

I got those boxed in back bog blues,
I know you heard them, they ain't nothin' new.
But if it's a crime to cry in your brew,
Somebody tell me what else I should do.

Crocodillies don't bother me,
I can't blame them for my misery,
It's just the climate of this swamp country,
I can't wait to get back home to Tennessee.

I need more than three squares and a bed,
I gots to take care of the state of my head,
If it weren't for snortin' an occasional red,
But I ain't sayin' that I wished I was dead.

I can't hitch-hike on no bayou bog,
The best friend I got's a tiny green frog,
If I had me a Ford or a Cadillac,
I'd be out of here and I would never come back.

I still remember those Nashville nights,
The drive-in movies and the honky tonk lights,
But there's one thing that worries me,
If I go back, who's gonna recognize me?

*(Repeat first verse)*

WORDS AND MUSIC BY SAM SHEPARD

*A shack in bayou swamp country. A wall of bare boards up-stage. A boarded up door center with a large window on either side of the door. On the walls are pictures of Jesus and assorted saints and crucifix. A table center stage with a Mexican type silk tablecloth with fringe. An oil lamp in the middle, hanging from the ceiling. Two chairs either side of the table and two mattresses, one against each wall, covered with Indian blankets. The stage is dark. Soft swamp noises; frogs, birds, bugs—then the shriek of a wildcat. A baby cries. The lights fade up softly. A pause as the baby continues to cry. A loud knocking at the door. Pause. The baby stops crying. Another series of knocks. MARIA, a dark-skinned woman with long straight black hair, a white cotton blouse, a long purple dress with red roses and a blue shawl with long fringe, comes on. She is very pregnant, has bare feet and carries a rifle. She squats down so she can't be seen through the windows from outside. More knocking. MARIA moves fast underneath the windows to the door and stands up, flattening her back against the door. A face appears in the stage left window, peering in. Then one appears in the stage right window. Both faces disappear. More knocking.*

**Maria**
Who is there!

**Slim's Voice**
It's the men you hired, ma'am!

**Maria**
What men!

**Slim's Voice**
The men from the high country!

**Maria**
What is my name?

**Slim's Voice**
Miss Maria, ma'am!

**Maria**
How much I pay you to come!

**Slim's Voice**
You ain't paid us nothin' so far, ma'am!

*MARIA unbolts the door and lets the two hired gunmen in: SLIM and SHADOW. SLIM is tall, he wears cowboy boots with spurs, jeans, a black satin shirt, a black leather jacket, a black cowboy hat with an Indian band, black leather gloves, and two pearl handled hand guns tied down to his hips. SHADOW is younger, shorter and darker skinned. He wears moccasins, brown leather pants, a flannel lumberjack shirt, a beaded vest, and a Sioux head band. He has one hand gun. They each carry rifles and packs over their shoulders. SLIM's rifle is a Winchester and SHADOW's is a sawed off shotgun.*

*MARIA quickly bolts the door behind them, then points her rifle at their heads. THEY raise their arms politely.*

**Slim**
Now, ma'am, there's no need to be so uppity. Don't you recognize us?

**Maria**
Come by light.

*She motions them over to the table and looks closely at their faces. She lowers the rifle.*

**Slim**
Now that's better. Nothin' to make a man feel less sure of himself than a woman pointin' a rifle at his head. Eh, Shadow?

*He jabs SHADOW with his elbow.*

**Shadow**
That's right, ma'am. Nothin!
**Maria**
You like coffee?
**Slim**
Now that would sure hit the spot, ma'am.
**Shadow**
Yeah, boy. And some fatback and biscuits if ya' got some.
   MARIA *nods and exits.*

   SLIM *and* SHADOW *look around the shack, then set their gear down on the floor and sit in the chairs,* SLIM *stage left and* SHADOW *stage right.* SHADOW *pulls out some chewing tobacco from his vest and offers it to* SLIM.

Care fer a little Red Man, Slim?
**Slim**
No thanks.
   SHADOW *bites off a hunk and chews as* SLIM *cases the joint with his eyes.*

Might as well've set ourselves up in a cracker box as try to defend this shack.
**Shadow**
How ya' mean? Seems simple enough. One of us each on a window and the woman coverin' the rear. Ain't no one gonna try comin' 'cross that back bog anyhow. And the front's clear.
**Slim**
Like I tried explainin' to ya' before, Shadow, it ain't no "one," no person, it's a "thing," a beast.
**Shadow**
Said yerself it was once a person, a man.
   *He spits a big gob of tobacco on the floor.*
**Slim**
It was. Maybe. Least that's what the woman said.
**Shadow**
Well, ain't there no way to tell?
**Slim**
We'll know soon enough.

**Shadow**
If it was a person once then chances are it'll still act like one.

**Slim**
We can't be countin' on that. We gotta get ourselves ready fer anything.

> MARIA *enters with a tray of coffee and biscuits.* SLIM *leaps to his feet and draws both pistols lightning fast.*

Oh. 'Scuse me, ma'am. Just keepin' on my toes. Gotta' make sure we earn our wages.

> MARIA *puts the tray down on the table.* SLIM *sits back down.*

**Shadow**
Speakin' a' wages, what is it you plan to pay us anyhow? Just out a' curiosity. My partner and I sorta' took the job out a' good faith, if ya' know what I mean.

**Maria**
I cannot pay you nothing.

**Shadow**
Now wait just a darn minute!

**Slim**
Hold on, Shadow.

**Maria**
But my man leaves me something.

> SHE *reaches in her blouse and pulls out a small gold wasp.*

**Slim**
Yer man? Well, where is he? How come he ain't here helpin' ya?

**Maria**
He is killed by the Tarpin.

**Slim**
Oh. Well, I'm sorry to hear that.

**Shadow**
What's the Tarpin?

> *He spits again.*

**Maria**
The pig beast. The beast kill my daughter. She about to

be a woman and the Tarpin kill her. My man go after pig beast and not come back. He leave me this. You take.

> SHADOW *takes the wasp from* MARIA *and holds it in his hand.*

**Shadow**

What's this here? Looks like a hornet or somethin'.

> *He bites it.*

Hm. Real gold, maybe. Can't be worth much though. This ain't even gonna pay fer horse fodder, Slim.

> *He spits on the floor.*

**Slim**

Shut up. Look, Maria, did you ever see the Tarpin?

**Maria**

Yes. I see.

**Slim**

Could ya' tell us what it looks like?

**Maria**

It is as big as man. Two heads.

**Shadow**

Two heads?

> *He spits again.*

**Slim**

Shut up, Shadow. And quit spittin' on the woman's floor.

**Maria**

Tusks like the wild boar.

**Slim**

Does it make any sound?

**Maria**

Snorts like a pig.

**Slim**

That's all?

**Maria**

Yes.

**Shadow**

Two heads. Sure.

**Maria**
It sometimes breathe fire. It have lights.
**Slim**
Lights? What kinda' lights?
**Maria**
Blue. Red. And gold.
**Slim**
Where do the lights come from?
**Maria**
The eyes. The head.
**Slim**
What's the body look like?
**Maria**
Thick brown skin. Like the pig. It is coming to kill my son.
**Slim**
How do you know that?
**Maria**
It has castrated all the sons in the lowland. My son is the last. It will kill my son. Then kill me.
**Slim**
Why you?
**Maria**
I am with child. It wants all children to die. All humans. It wants to stop our race.
**Slim**
How do you know that?
**Maria**
It tell me.
**Slim**
It spoke to you?
**Shadow**
She ain't playing with a full deck.
**Slim**
Maria, it spoke to you, the beast?

**Maria**
Yes.
**Slim**
How? Did it use words?
**Maria**
It speak through my brain.
**Slim**
In English?
**Maria**
In Cajun.
**Slim**
Are you Cajun?
**Maria**
No.
**Slim**
Then how do you know it was Cajun?
**Maria**
You are from high country. You do not know the ways of the lowland. It speak in Cajun.
> MARIA *exits.*

**Shadow**
Well, what do ya' make a' that?
> *He spits again.*

**Slim**
She's telling the truth.
**Shadow**
So you really think there's a beast out there?
**Slim**
Listen, I never been in this part a' the country before but I can tell ya' one thing. It weren't no human being that burned off that land that we come across. Not even a stick a' shrub pine left. It's gotta be some kinda' beast that'd do a thing like that. All them antelope with their bellies ripped out. What hunger you ever seen leaves a carcass layin' like that?
**Shadow**
Ya' got me, Slim. How come she says it talks though?

**Slim**

Can't figure that out myself. Unless it's some kinda' mental telepathy like the Arapaho have.

**Shadow**

Maybe it is an Arapaho in some kinda' crazy costume. A renegade gone loco.

**Slim**

Not this far south. Nope, it's somethin' bigger and spookier than you or me can reckon to. Somethin's goin' on down here, Shadow. Somethin' horrible's goin' on.

**Shadow**

Well, it ain't bad coffee the woman makes. I say we stick it out a couple days and rest up. Get some good grits in our gullets and move on. We can't be hangin' around just waitin' fer the damn thing to turn up.

**Slim**

Didn't you hear what she said, Shadow? That Tarpin beast means to annihilate the human race. That's you and me, boy. It starts with the kids. Kills them off one at a time. All the kids. The boys. You know what that means? No boys—no men. No men—no babies. No babies—no people. Do you remember seein' one living soul the whole time since we crossed over from the high country? Not a one. This woman and her baby boy and her unborn in her belly are the last living things in this neck of the woods. And once it finishes with its dirty work here it's gonna move on. Move north. To the high country.

**Shadow**

Well, you know me, Slim. I only took to this hired gun racket recently. Doggin' bulls was my specialty. The only reason I took up with ya' was 'cause I thought I'd make myself a tad more money. I never expected ya' to go in fer no heroism.

**Slim**

It ain't heroism! Golldangit, Shadow! Come down to earth, boy. It's pure and simple survival. It's either us or him.

**Shadow**

"It."

**Slim**

"Him," "it," what's the difference. We're gonna have to do somethin' about it sooner or later. It might as well be now. Better than goin' back home to the ranch and waitin' for it to come terrorizin' the wife and kids.

**Shadow**

What wife and kids! What ranch! Come down to earth yer own self.

**Slim**

I told ya' about my dreams, Shadow. Now don't begrudge me that. A man can dream, can't he?

**Shadow**

Sure, but not all the goddam time. Ya' can't always be walkin' around like a woman in love.

**Slim**

And ya' can't be walkin' around like a mad dog kicked out in the cold, neither. I've had my fill a' lonely campfires and beans from a can. I want somethin' more. I'm gettin' on in years, Shadow. You, you're still young and wirey. You could always go back to bulldoggin' if ya' hankered to. Not me. There was a time when the speed a' these two six guns was all the security I needed. Now, I've lost a good tenth of a second or more. Sometimes even the right draws faster than the left. There was a time last month when I even got my thumb stuck on the hammer. Things like that make a man start to wonder. I have nightmares a' bein' gunned down on the street by some a' these hot shot young dudes that a' been sproutin' up.

**Shadow**

Shh! What's that?

> *They both snap into action and duck down behind their chairs. They listen. Silence.*

**Slim**

What? I don't hear nothin'.

**Shadow**

Shh!

> *They listen again. A scraping sound comes from outside,*
> *then a moan. They signal to each other, then quickly crawl*
> *over to underneath the windows. They listen. Again the*
> *scraping and the moan. SHADOW whips out a knife and*
> *signals to SLIM. SLIM slowly, carefully reaches over to the*
> *bolt on the door. A pause. SHADOW nods, then suddenly*
> *SLIM unbolts the door and yanks it open.*

> *An old PREACHER with a long grey beard and a clerical*
> *collar staggers in. He is dressed like an Amish priest and*
> *covered with blood, his clothes ripped and slashed. SHADOW*
> *grabs him from behind and holds the knife to his throat.*
> *SLIM slams the door shut and bolts it. The PREACHER is*
> *dazed.*

State yer business, old timer.

**Slim**

Hold it, Shadow. Can't ya' see he's injured? What's the matter with you?

> *SHADOW loosens his grip and puts the knife away. SLIM*
> *helps the PREACHER over to the table and lays him down*
> *on it.*

Come on now. It's all right. No one's gonna hurt ya'. Jest lay yerself down there. Come on. That's it.

> *SLIM lays the PREACHER on his back across the table with*
> *his arms and legs hanging over the edge.*

Shadow, get Maria. See if she's got any whiskey and some boiling water.

> *SHADOW exits. SLIM starts ripping the Preacher's shirt off.*

Just take her easy there, mister. We'll see to what ails ya'. That's right. Breathe deep. There ya' go.

> *The PREACHER speaks as he struggles to sit up while SLIM*
> *pushes him back down.*

**Preacher**

Take courage, my children, cry to God and he will deliver you from the power and hand of the enemy!

**Slim**

Jest settle down, mister. No one's gonna hurt ya'. Take it easy.

**Preacher**

My children, endure with patience the wrath that has come upon you from God. Your enemies have overtaken you, but you will soon see their destruction and will tread upon their necks!

**Slim**

Shadow! Hurry it up!

**Preacher**

They shall be wasted with hunger and devoured with burning heat and poisonous pestilence, and I will send the teeth of beasts against them, with venom of crawling things of the dust!

**Slim**

Shadow!

**Preacher**

Then the earth reeled and rocked; the foundations of the heavens trembled and quaked, because he was angry! Smoke went up from his nostrils, and devouring fire from his mouth; glowing coals flamed forth from him! He bowed the heavens and came down; thick darkness was under his feet! He rode on a cherub and flew; he was seen upon the wings of the wind! He made darkness around him his canopy, thick clouds, a gathering of water! Out of the brightness before him coals of fire flamed forth! The Lord thundered from heaven and the Most High uttered his voice! And he sent out arrows and scattered them; lightning, and routed them! Then the channels of the sea were seen, the foundations of the world were laid bare, at the rebuke of the Lord, at the blast of the breath of his nostrils!

> *The* PREACHER *falls back into a comatose state as* SHADOW *enters with* MARIA *carrying a bottle of whiskey and some hot water in a bowl.*

**Slim**

Well, it's about goddamn time. Never cottoned too much to sermons ever since I was a kid.

**Maria**
Who this man?
**Slim**
Search me, ma'am. He's wounded pretty bad though. Looks like that beast done it. He'd probably be beholdin' to ya' if ya' fixed him up some.
**Maria**
I no tell you to let strangers in.
**Shadow**
We thought he was that pig-beast, ma'am.
**Maria**
Pig? He no pig.
**Shadow**
I know, but we thought. . . .
**Slim**
Never mind, Shadow. Look, ma'am, if ya' don't mind, we're a little tuckered from the ride—could we just make use of yer mattresses?
**Maria**
Yes. Sleep. I wake you up.
> MARIA *rips off the* PREACHER's *shirt and dresses his wound.*
> SLIM *goes to the stage right mattress and gets ready for bed.*
**Shadow**
Well, that's a fine how do you do. Here I'm all riled up about pig beasts and the annihilation a' the human race and you wants to sleep.
**Slim**
Suit yerself, boy. Here's an old man talkin'.
**Shadow**
Ya' want a bennie or a red or somethin', Slim?
**Slim**
Sorry. Don't go in fer dope much. Straight whiskey's my nemesis.
**Shadow**
Well, here.
> *He grabs the bottle from* MARIA *and offers it to* SLIM.

Let's have us a little celebration on the successful cross-
ing of the fearsome lowlands without one single tangle
with the much heard about but seldom seen pig-beast.

**Maria**

That medicine. No for drink.

> *She grabs the bottle back and goes on with tending to the*
> PREACHER.

**Slim**

Listen, boy, we was hired to do a job. That job depends on
us bein' fit and able. Now I ain't one to get in the way of
a man's pleasures, but when it starts goin' contrary to the
best interests of. . . .

**Shadow**

All right! I don't need no lecture. Go ahead and flake out.
I'm takin' a walk in the moonlight. There any pretty young
Cajun babes out there in the woods yearnin' fer the likes
a' me, Maria?

**Maria**

No Cajun.

**Shadow**

Yeah, O.K. Just thought I'd check. Well, see ya'all later
on.

> *He picks up his rifle and goes out the door.*

**Slim**

Don't get ate up now!

> MARIA *crosses quickly to the door and bolts it.* SLIM *has his*
> *boots and guns off. He takes off his pants, revealing long*
> *john underwear underneath. He crawls under the covers.*
> MARIA *goes back to the* PREACHER.

How's the old goat doin'?

**Maria**

Goat?

**Slim**

The preacher man. Think he'll pull through?

> MARIA *doesn't answer.*

You don't savvy even half a' what I'm sayin', do ya'?

> *Pause.*

How would ye' like a little roll in the old sack, baby?
> MARIA *keeps dressing the* PREACHER's *wounds.*

How 'bout suckin' on my ding-dong or somethin'? Talkin'
thataway makes me feel almost as young as that Shadow
boy. Almost. Bet you knocked 'em dead when you was
nineteen, didn't ya', Maria?

**Maria**

Yes?

**Slim**

Nothin'. I'll just bet you had 'em lined up though. Yessir.
A regular Mardi Gras Cajun queen. Funny you'd wind
up way out here like this. On the lam. Runnin' scared. Too
bad about yer old man. Must a' been a nice fella'. Hell
of a way to go. Gettin' ate alive like that. That is the way
he does it, ain't it? Must be. Horrible death. Me, I always
think about dyin' by the gun. You know, like in the Bible.
He who lives by the sword and all that malarkey. Still, it's
true. There's some young whipper snapper out there just
waitin'. Just practicin' and practicin' on old soup cans
and waitin' to put another notch on his six gun. 'Course
he don't know it's gonna be me. We ain't never met personally. I don't really have no enemies 'cause I killed 'em
all. Most of 'em wasn't even my own enemies. They was
somebody else's. Still they're all dead and that's a good
feelin', knowin' there ain't no one doggin' ya' night and
day just to plug ya' in the backside. Ain't got no out-
standin' debts neither. Guess I owe Shadow a nickel or
two from poker and beer but that's about it. Don't owe no
man nothin'. Guess you don't neither, do ya', Maria?

**Maria**

Yes?

> *The baby starts to cry softly in the next room.* MARIA *exits.*
> *The* PREACHER *lies unconscious on the table as* SLIM *keeps*
> *talking.*

**Slim**

Guess not. Still it get lonely just draggin' around from
one two-bit town to the next. Lookin' fer people with enemies. Enemies and money is all I need to stay in business.

Most of my clients are just plain cowards. Cowards or women or rich gentlemen from Boston that never learned to even holster a six gun, let alone shoot the damn thing. Bankers and financiers and loan sharks. Men who make the country run. Not like me. Me, I'm out to make a few bucks. Save up a roll fer the ranch. The wife and kids. Keep the belly warm. It's no good bein' homeless, ya' know. It eats at a man from the inside out. Ya' wonder where all the people went. At night. They go away from ya'. They got fires and warmth inside. Outside the world swallows a man up. He gets lost in it. There's no end to it. He starts cravin' fer some warmth like a hungry dog. Fer a lover, a friend.

*The lamp and the lights start dimming softly.*

Just some conversation. That's sorta' why I hitched up with that Shadow boy. Just so's I could ramble on to some human being instead a' that damn pinto or the sage brush. I ain't alone though. I know that much. I ain't to be pitied no more than the rest of 'em out there. No more than this old preacher man. Hey, preacher man? I bet you got stories to tell. And the rest of 'em out there. That Shadow boy out there in the night with his heart poundin' just from bein' born. Just from the moon and the stars. I can still remember how that felt. To still feel part of the earth. Lost in all that space but not givin' a goddamn 'cause it meant you was free. Free to be alive. I can feel myself growin'. Not older, just growin'. Growin' outwards.

*The lights fade to black. Soft blue light comes up on the side of the stage. The* GHOST *of* MARIA's *dead daughter appears dressed in a long blue gypsy dress. She sings.*

## LOWLANDS

*Chorus:*
Lowlands, lowlands, heave away, Joe.

I had a dream the other night.
'Bout a dollar and a dime a day.

Dreamed that the earth was sunk into the sea.
'Bout a dollar and a dime a day.

*(Chorus)*

Blue was the only color we could see
At a dollar and a dime a day.
Nothing but ship and star and sea
At a dollar and a dime a day.

*(Chorus)*

Hope that was just a dream I had
At a dollar and a dime a day,
If you don't drown the sea will drive you mad,
At a dollar and a dime a day.

*(Chorus)*

TRADITIONAL
NEW WORDS BY STEVE WEBER AND ANTONIA

*Cross fade to stage.*

## Scene 2:

*The lights come back up to morning light. The PREACHER is still on the table, SLIM is still in bed. SHADOW's VOICE from outside.*

**Shadow's Voice**

Rise and shine! Rise and shine!

*More banging. The sound of a girl giggling along with SHADOW.*

Every man to his post! The place is surrounded with pig-beasts! Every man to his station!

*SLIM suddenly rolls out of his bed across the floor with both pistols in his hands, at the ready. More banging.*

Shake a leg in there! Slim! The sun's been up for hours!

*SLIM gets up, goes to the door and opens it. SHADOW enters with GRIS GRIS, a young girl with long black hair and a long purple dress. She wears big gold earrings, rings on every finger, necklaces around her neck. SHADOW and GRIS GRIS have their arms full of large yellow mushrooms. SLIM locks the door behind them.*

Good morning, old scout. This here is Gris Gris.

**Slim**
Mornin'.

**Shadow**
We picked ya' some breakfast. All we need is some hot boilin' water in a kettle and we're in business.

**Gris Gris**
Ya' *fry* mushrooms, ya' don't boil 'em. Ya' fry frog legs. Ya' fry fish eyes. Ya' fry water moccasins. Ya' fry everything down here. Ya' fry men sometimes.

**Slim**
Looks like you got yerself a live one there.

**Shadow**
What's the old preacher man still doin' here? He's blockin' up our breakfast table.

**Slim**
Where'd ya' expect him to spend the night?

**Shadow**
Well, it ain't night time no longer. It's time he moseyed on. Come on, Gris Gris, set these over here.
> *They go to the other mattress stage left and dump the mushrooms on it.*

Come on, Slim. Help me move this old dude off the breakfast table.

**Slim**
Leave him be, Shadow. He had a rough day.
> SHADOW *hoists the* PREACHER *up on his shoulder and lifts him off the table. The* PREACHER *starts to babble again.* SHADOW *can't decide where to put him.*

**Shadow**
Come on now, Lazarus.

**Preacher**
The Lord has set the sun in the heavens, but has said that he would dwell in thick darkness. I have built thee an exalted house, a place for thee to dwell in forever.

**Shadow**
Well, it ain't this house, brother. It's crowded enough as

it is. Gris Gris, move them mushrooms out a' the way
there.

> GRIS GRIS *moves all the mushrooms from the bed over to
> the table.* SHADOW *flops the* PREACHER *down on the mat-
> tress.*

**Preacher**
He boasted that he would burn up my territory and kill
my young men with the sword and dash my infants to
the ground and seize my children as prey, and take my
virgins as booty!

**Shadow**
Aw, pipe down, ya' old stomper.

**Gris Gris**
Who's he?

**Shadow**
Some old Bible thumper the wind blew in.

> GRIS GRIS *takes out a long knife from her boot and starts
> cutting up the mushrooms on the table.* SHADOW *kisses
> her on the cheek. She giggles.* SLIM *is getting dressed.*

**Preacher**
Then my oppressed people shouted for joy; for weak
people shouted and the enemy trembled; they lifted up
their voices and the enemy were turned back! The sons
of maidservants have pierced them through; they were
wounded like the children of fugitives, they perished before the army of my Lord!

**Shadow**
Sure does know his Bible, don't he?

**Slim**
Ye'r gonna be old one day yerself, smart ass.

**Shadow**
But I ain't gonna be unconscious one minute and runnin' off at the mouth the next.

**Preacher**
Woe to the nations that rise up against my people. The
Lord almighty will take vengeance on them in the day of

judgment . . . fire and worms he will give to their flesh!
They shall weep in pain forever!

**Gris Gris**

Your ass. Who is this zombie, anyway?

**Shadow**

I don't know.

**Gris Gris**

Why don't you kick him out? He's takin' up my oxygen.

**Slim**

Look, girl, you just arrived here and ya' might have some
respect for an older man.

**Gris Gris**

I might. I might get down on my knees and eat worms
too but I ain't gonna.

**Slim**

Where'd you find this one, boy?

**Shadow**

Ain't she somethin'?

**Slim**

Y'all plannin' on eatin' this poison?

**Shadow**

Sure. Gris Gris here knows how to tell the good ones
from the bad. Dontcha', girl?

**Gris Gris**

Sometimes. Sometimes I make mistakes and get the
scuzzy ones. The dark ones. The ones with blood stains
marked on the rim.

**Shadow**

Shoulda' seen it, Slim. A whole mountain full of these yellow buttons. Looked like a poppy field from a distance,
but Gris Gris knew right off they was magic mushrooms.
. . . Didn't ya, girl?

**Slim**

What mountain? There ain't no mountain. I wouldn't
touch them things with a ten-foot pole.

> MARIA *enters.*

**Maria**
Who this girl?
**Shadow**
This here's Gris Gris, ma'am.
**Maria**
You eat, then go.
**Shadow**
Now that ain't very neighborly.
**Slim**
She's a swamp girl, Shadow. She belongs in the swamp.
**Shadow**
You belong in the zoo, old man.
**Slim**
You can't talk to me like that and get away with it.
**Shadow**
Ya' wanna' go fer yer gun, old man?
**Maria**
No fight! This is peaceful home. No fight. I fix breakfast,
then these two go.
**Slim**
I don't think the preacher's ready yet, ma'am. He's still
babblin' on about God and such.
**Maria**
You wake him up for to eat.
**Shadow**
We picked ya' some nice fresh mushrooms, ma'am. How
'bout puttin' 'em in a skillet for us?
**Maria**
Where you get these?
**Slim**
Says they found 'em on top of a mountain. Now you tell
me, Maria, is there a mountain anywhere near here?
**Maria**
No mountain.
**Slim**
There. What'd I tell ya'.

**Shadow**

Well, I guess it's our word against yours. And here's the evidence sittin' right here on the table.

**Slim**

That don't mean nothin'. Ya' coulda' picked mushrooms anywheres. Maybe they belong to that pig-beast. Maria, you ever seen mushrooms like these here?

**Maria**

Not so big. So yellow. They bad poison. Black magic.

**Gris Gris**

Black as the inside of a dog's mouth. Black enough to burn holes through your skull. Black, black, black!

**Slim**

I say they're beast bait, somethin' that beast put out there to trick us into eatin'.

**Maria**

Then we all die.

**Gris Gris**

And our ghosts are taken by the voodoo man. And our souls are stripped down and licked clean by the sons of Osimandias.

> *She plays her fiddle.*

**Shadow**

Well, Gris Gris and I'll eat 'em then and you two can have ham and eggs. That way if we die there'll still be two of ya' left to fight off the beast.

**Slim**

No dice, Shadow. We're gonna need every gun we can muster up when that beast decides to come through the door.

**Shadow**

Goddamnit, we picked 'em and we're gonna' eat 'em!

**Slim**

Shadow, fer once in yer young life listen to reason. Now I been around some and I learned how to smell out a trap or two in my time. This mushroom business smells mighty peculiar. Now first off ya' tell me ya' find these here toadstools on top of a mountain and there just ain't no mountains around here. Second of all—

**Shadow**

Me and Gris Gris here is eatin' these mushrooms fer breakfast, Slim. And if you aim to stop us yer gonna' have to kill us.

**Maria**

No fight here. Fight outside.

**Shadow**

Anywhere ya' want it.

> *A pause as SLIM and SHADOW face each other off. SLIM breaks the tension by going to the PREACHER.*

**Slim**

Guess I'll try wakin' up the old geezer. Lord knows he could use somethin' in that belly after all he's been through.

**Shadow**

Gris Gris, why don't you and Maria go in the kitchen and fetch us a skillet so we can get to fryin' these things. Go on.

**Gris Gris**

Come on, Mama Reux. Let's see what you got in your kitchen. Let's cook up a potion for these dudes.

> *SHADOW picks up a piece of the mushrom and smells it. He pops it into his mouth and chews. He sits on the table and keeps popping pieces of mushroom into his mouth and watching SLIM, whose back is to him as he tries to wake up the PREACHER.*

**Slim**

Come on, old timer. Time to face a new day.

**Shadow**

Never figured you to be one to back down, Slim. Least not from a bulldogger like me.

**Slim**

> *To the PREACHER.*

Come on, now. Get some hot breakfast in yer belly and you'll be a new man.

**Shadow**

Me, I couldn't go on livin' with a fear like that. No sir. That kind of uncertainty about yerself. I'd rather die a fool than back down in front a' women folk like that.

**Slim**

Jest open yer eyes and take a big yawn. Come on. Can't sleep the whole day away.

**Shadow**

'Course now, it just may be that you was takin' pity on me. Just may be that. Knew you was faster all along. Takes a lot a' courage to turn the other cheek. Don't it?

> SLIM *wheels around and knocks* SHADOW *off the table onto the floor. He gets on top of him and straddles his chest, pinning his arms to the ground.*

**Slim**

Now listen, you saddle tramp no 'count. The only reason I took you on was 'cause I was tired a' makin' it alone. If I needed a fast gun I could a' had my pick a' the best. Plus, I felt sorry for ya'. Sittin' around whittlin' on fence posts; carvin' yer initials in bar stools. Let me tell you somethin', boy. Now you listen good. Don't you ever push me again. You hear? Not never. 'Cause I'll blast you wide open like a bale a' sawdust.

> The PREACHER *suddenly sits up on the mattress and looks around as though waking up from a long sleep.* SLIM *and* SHADOW *relax and watch him. The* PREACHER *stands up and walks across the room. He stops and looks around. He sees the mushrooms on the table and walks over to them. He picks one up and eats it.* SLIM *stands.*

Wait a minute. Don't eat them things. Them's beast bait.

> The PREACHER *smiles. He speaks as though talking to no one in particular.*

**Preacher**

And the Lord said to Moses and Aaron, "Say to the people of Israel, These are the living things which you may eat among all the beasts that are on the earth. Whatever parts the hoof and is cloven-footed and chews the cud, among the animals, you may eat. And the swine, because it parts the hoof and is cloven-footed but does not chew the cud, is unclean to you. Of their flesh you shall not eat, and their carcasses you shall not touch; they are unclean to you."

> The PREACHER *crosses back to the mattress and lies down and goes back into a trance state.*

**Slim**

Now if that don't beat all.

> SHADOW *gets up off the floor.*

**Shadow**

I say we turn him back out. He ain't right in the head, Slim.

**Slim**

You wouldn't be neither if that beast had grabbed you out there.

**Shadow**

There ain't no beast! Maria's made it all up. I'm tellin' ya', me and Gris Gris tramped all around out there last night and the worst thing we seen was a hoot owl with a water snake wrapped around its beak.

> GRIS GRIS *enters playing her fiddle. As she enters the room,* SHADOW *doubles over in pain, clutching his stomach and moaning.*

**Slim**

Shadow, boy!

**Gris Gris**

My fiddle plays a death song. I sing it through my ears. Frogs move in me. Crawdaddies play with my soul. Something moves my fingers over strings. Something strikes the bow like a torch.

**Slim**

It's them damn toadstools! . . . Come on!

> GRIS GRIS *makes no move to help but keeps playing her fiddle like a death chant.* SLIM *pulls* SHADOW *over to the stage right mattress and flops him down.*

**Gris Gris**

You zombies rip me up. Your death walk. Death stance.

Staring into what you can't see. Take me, not the night.
Turn your back on the beast. But you can't. He's close
now. His breath breathes your breath. You are him. He's
in you.

**Slim**

You put a spell on him! You're nothin' but a demon
witch!

**Gris Gris**

Spells are meant to be broken. But you're locked in.
You got no keys. You got no gris gris. You got no magic
to use. Well, let me give you some. I'll pass it around.
There's stuff to spare in the air. Take it. Take some mojo
root jam. Some John the Conqueroot jam. Some toad
skin. Some fish tooth. Some cocoa leaf juice. Some
swamp gas. Moss blood. Anything is useful. Use your
dirty socks if you can find your feet.

**Slim**

Maria!

**Gris Gris**

And don't think he ain't comin' 'cause I called him up.
I talked to his teeth and he answers like the owl. He's
hootin' out for this shack. This little pile of sticks. We're
all gonna burn at his stake. So get ready to see through
fire. Get set to smell flesh. Signify on your knees if you
got the balls. 'Cause snakes is gonna slither on your
zombie corpse!

> *During this,* SHADOW *has been going through convulsions,*
> *with* SLIM *trying to hold him down. When* GRIS GRIS *finishes,*
> SHADOW *collapses.* SLIM *covers him with the blanket, then*
> *turns to* GRIS GRIS.

**Slim**

You poisoned him.

**Gris Gris**

Poison's in the air, Jack. Some people take it, some
leave it.

**Slim**

You poisoned him with them toadstools. You knew they
was poison. Shadow was my right hand man. So now you

gotta look to your left. A left handed gunman. Now that's something to strut your stuff about. None a' this candy cock side kick shit. Use your left, baby. Look to your left. Watch out!

> SLIM *wheels and draws to his left side as though about to fire at an unseen gunman.*

**Gris Gris**

There he is! Lurkin' in the Spanish moss. A dark black moustache man crouched in the leaves, crawling through the ferns with a knife gleaming 'tween his jagged teeth. He's out for you like a swamp dog smellin' coon blood. Your time is comin', cowboy.

**Slim**

No! I done him in in Nogales. No! It was Santa Fe. No! Elko, Nevada. That was it. I finished him. I remember his face. His teeth were gushin' blood. He ain't comin'.

**Gris Gris**

There's another one! Watch it now!

> SLIM *wheels again drawing his gun.*

He slinks, this one. He preys on wounded knees. He knows your hat size. He's followed your saloon trail. He knows your boot prints backwards.

**Slim**

Not him! I got him good. Two chambers and he still kept comin'. But he died at my feet. At my feet! He kissed my boot! He kissed it and thanked me for it! I remember you! All month, trackin' through powder snow. Found him in a pine ridge. Not that one! He's gone! Gone, I tell ya'!

**Gris Gris**

There's more out there. More shadows.

**Slim**

Nothin', I tell ya'! They all been done! No one's comin' but some beast we don't even know about! I'll tell ya' another thing. I dealt with witches before. You ain't the first. You ain't got no power over this fox, honey. I'm goin' out there. I'm goin' out there to find this here mysterious mountain you conjured up. And if I find it I'm gonna tear it down. With my bare hands. I'm gonna make a rumble that they won't stop hearin' till the low-lands falls into the sea! Then I'm comin' back for you and you best be ready. 'Cause no one puts a spell on this dude. No one! You hear?

**Gris Gris**

Good luck.

> SLIM *exits.* GRIS GRIS *crosses between the* PREACHER *and* SHADOW. *She looks them over and says a prayer.*

She danced with a fish held high over her head. She breathed to the moon. The village killed her. Cut off her head and dropped it down a well. That spring all the people died from drinking the water.

> MARIA *enters.*

**Maria**

What happened to this man?

**Gris Gris**

He's drunk on air. Maybe you could pull some white charms out of your basket. Do him good.

**Maria**

How he get sick?

**Gris Gris**

You must know some magic, Mama. Let's put the powers into play. Let's dance a dance. A spirit dance over this poor bull doggin' fool. You take the right, I'll take the left. You take the white, I'll take the black. It's a little contest. You wanna play?

**Maria**

He very sick?

**Gris Gris**

Very sick. He needs a sycamore syringe up his ass.

**Maria**

I help.

**Gris Gris**

Good. Then let the voodoo come!

> MARIA *bends down over* SHADOW *and begins a ritual to exorcize his demons.* GRIS GRIS *goes to stage left and*

*plays high wailing screeches on the fiddle and tries to possess* SHADOW *with the demons.* MARIA *hums softly.*

In the heart of a mongoose the Lowlands prayed for rain. Rain in the tropics. The Cajuns clacked their teeth. The swamps dried up into cracked mud. Dead snapping turtles lay on their backs baking in the sun. Fish floated on the sand. The rocks turned green. The mystery was real and all the people felt the presence of the beast. Some say they saw him coming in their dreams. Dream language came out of their mouths. Symbols were seen in the shapes of clouds. Dust hung over their homes. A desert was growing. Coyotes took the place of the Blue Tipped Coon Hound. Howls broke branches in the night.

*During this,* SHADOW *begins to have tremors conflicting between the magic of* MARIA *and* GRIS GRIS.

Women covered their heads with black sacks with eyes cut like the slit eyes of a wolf. Men covered their mouths. Horses fell in the fields and went stiff with their hooves pointed toward the sun. The sky went black, then changed to white like a photograph of death. The crocodile dives to deeper water, touches bottom, crawls along the muddy bottom, hides his ears from the sound of the land. The stink moves from east to west, then changes wind and moves back again. Their noses are on fire. The eyes water and cause moss to grow on their cheeks. Everywhere the people move in bands of a dozen or less. Breaking up, coming together. Screaming crazy, throwing themselves on their own campfires. Eating the flames. The beast has come.

*The two heads of the pig-beast appear in the stage left window. No sound.* GRIS GRIS *and* MARIA *have their backs to the window and don't notice. Just the audience sees it. It peers in, then disappears, then reappears in the stage right window and disappears again.* GRIS GRIS *continues.*

He moves in their thoughts. Tracks them running. Tracks them walking. Tracks them sleeping. Blocks their escape. Tortures their minds with no hope. Drags them down in the bayou mud. Boils their eyes. Crosses their vision. Doubles their senses. Eats them raw and spits them back.

> SHADOW *begins to writhe and scream.* MARIA *keeps up her ritual.* GRIS GRIS *is relentless, wailing on her fiddle and screaming into the air.*

Blood rains from the sky. The earth opens up and swallows them whole. The sky rips and tears like a paper bag. Carcasses turn into tumbleweeds. The wind blows them back to the sea. The sea bellows the voice of the beast. It rips up the trees and throws them down like broken ships. The sea evens out into a flat green glassy shine and smiles at its dirty work. The beast cackles like the jackal and broken things bob on the surface. The moon sinks behind the sun and the sun shines black. The beast has come. The beast has come. The beast has come.

> SHADOW *goes limp and lifeless.* MARIA *rises slowly. She takes a moment and looks at* GRIS GRIS, *then exits.* GRIS GRIS *stares out over the audience, then slowly opens her mouth and makes a silent scream.* MARIA, *at the very moment* GRIS GRIS *opens her mouth, screams from off stage.* MARIA *enters, hands dripping with blood.*

**Maria**

My son! My boy is dead!

## BLACKOUT

*During blackout* GHOST GIRL *is heard singing "Wrap Your Troubles in Dreams."*

**Scene 3:**

Wrap your troubles in dreams
Send them all away
Put them in a bottle and
Across the sea they'll stay

Speak not of misfortune
Speak not of your woes
Just steal yourself a holy death
Crouching by the door

Writhe and sway to music's pain
Searing with asides
Caress death with a lover's touch
And it shall be your bride

Purple is to yellow as
Sunlight is to rain

Happiness in death you'll find
Loveliness in pain

Slash the golden whip it snaps
Across the lover's sides
The earth trembles without remorse
Preparing for to die

Salty ocean waves and sprays
Come crashing to the shore
Bullies kick and kill young loves
Down on bar room floors

The gleaming knife cuts early
Through the midnight air
Cutting entrails in its path
Blood runs without care

Violence echoes through the land
And heart of every man
The knife it stabs existent wounds
Pus runs through matted hair

Excrement filters through the brain
Hatred bends the spine
Filth covers the body pores
To be cleansed by dying time

WORDS AND MUSIC BY LOU REED

*As song is ended, the lights come up slowly on* SHADOW *and the* PREACHER *on different sides of the stage. They are both coming out of their respective spells, the rhythms of their language and action shifting from one side of the stage to the other. They are the only two on stage.*

**Shadow**
Gimme a good bull! That's all I'm askin'! A good bull! All I need's a good ride! Just one good ride! That's all I'm askin'! Gimme the Twister or Buttermilk or the

Monsoon! Any a' them! Gimme somethin' with some
heart in him!

**Preacher**

Now you kids be back before dusk and don't be bringin'
back no slimey things. Empty your pockets out 'fore
you come in the door. You hear? Stay away from the
black folk. You cross the tracks and you'll get a
whoopin' sure as I'm born. I seen you playin' with
black Willie. I seen you. Now don't lie to me! Don't
you lie or the Lord'll paddle yer blue jeans off.

**Shadow**

Tucson. Couldn't make it in a day anyhow. Could
hitch-hike out to Omaha. Tuba city. The damn circuit.
They don't make the circuit for a poorboy. Every cow-
puncher come along thinks he's a star right off. Just
off the range. Shoulda' stuck with stock cars. Get a
damn Ford out there. Don't gotta depend on no bull.
Every Brahma's different. Stick to bulldoggin'. Never
can tell. Not like a damn Ford. Just stomp it. 'At's it.
Ata' boy. Slipstream the mother.

**Preacher**

The bobwhite says "Bob White." The whippoorwill says
"Whip poor will." We could put a message in a White
Lightning bottle and send it to a faraway place. Just
toss it in the Gulf a' Mexico. No tellin' who'd find it. We
could write a joke. Like "Who Killed Cock Robin."

*In another voice.*

You boys get on away from them skiffs. Get on, ya'
hear! Go catch yerselves some catfish. Make yerself
useful.

*Another voice.*

Let's play the jukebox down at Jango's place.

*Another voice.*

I don't like Jango. Last time he tried to whoop me fer
stealin' sugar.

**Shadow**

Least in football ya' got all that paddin'. All that cushion.

More bones broke in a rodeo than ever was in football. Let me see the nurse. The head nurse. They got no right holdin' me here against my will. I gotta earn me a livin'. I ain't gonna go into traction neither. I don't care. I'll ride a damn Brahma with two legs broke and my collar bone flappin'. I don't give a damn. Lemme see the doctor. It's *my* leg, ain't it? Nobody else's. It's my neck.

**Preacher**
Remember that Packard used to set out in front of Sukie's garage? That thing was so beautiful. I used to walk past there thinkin' about the shine on them fenders. I used to look at my teeth in that paint job and just grin and grin. Well, one day I stole it. That's right. I couldn't believe it. There it was just settin' there with the engine hummin' and the keys in it and everything. And I just hopped in the son of a bitch and took off. Drove and drove like a crazy man. Finally got it stuck in a bog. I just left it there. I just laughed and laughed and left it there.

**Shadow**
They never tell ya the worst. A man's got a right to know. It's my life, ain't it? Don't let 'em take my leg off no matter what. They'll have to shoot me first. They'll have to shoot me.

> *Loud banging on the door. Outside* SLIM *is heard bellowing.*

**Slim's Voice**
All right. Open up in there. What's going on?

> *More loud banging.* SHADOW *and the* PREACHER *lie motionless.*

Open up, I tell ya'! It's me! Slim! What the hell's goin' on? Open up this door 'fore I bust it down!

> *More banging as* MARIA *enters from the kitchen. She goes to the door and opens it slowly.* SLIM *enters.* MARIA *bolts the door behind him.*

**Slim**
What's goin' on, Maria? Didn't ya' hear me out there?

**Maria**
My son is dead.

**Slim**
Dead? What do you mean?

**Maria**
That beast kill my son.

**Slim**
The beast? He was here? Now look, Maria, I been walkin' all over tarnation out there and I didn't see no sign a' no beast. Are you sure you're telling the truth about this whole thing?

**Maria**
The beast come. My boy is dead.

**Slim**
You know what I think? I think it's that damn swamp gypsy. I think she's at the root a' this beast thing. Where is she anyhow? Maria?

**Maria**
My boy is dead.

**Slim**
I know that. And I'm sorry. There ain't nothin' I can do about it now. We gotta find that swamp girl and find out the truth about what's goin' on or we're all gonna be dead. Now where is she?

**Maria**
She gone.

**Slim**
Well, where'd she go?

**Maria**
She vanish.

**Slim**
All right now, can the mumbo jumbo! I'm sick and tired a' all this fool magic stuff and visions flying around. Now where'd she go?

> GRIS GRIS *enters from the kitchen playing her fiddle gently. She saunters onto the stage.*

**Gris Gris**
You lookin' fer me, cowboy?

**Maria**
No! You go back. You hide.

**Gris Gris**
I'll hide when there's somethin' to fear, Maria. Right now I'm naked as a snake.

**Slim**
Now you look here, girl. I don't know what yer game is, but you best come out with the truth or I'll be forced to take drastic measures.

**Gris Gris**
You gonna stake me out in the sun and pour red ants down my ears?

**Maria**
She knows nothing. She is Cajun girl. She is strange to you.

**Slim**
She's strange all right. Strange enough to send me on a wild goose chase looking for a mountain full a' yellow mushrooms. Strange enough to put a spell on my partner here. Strange enough to conjure up some beast that don't exist. Now ain't that the truth? You been lying all along? Maria, is she the one who first told you about the beast?

**Maria**
No.

**Slim**
Well, who did then?

**Maria**
We know. The Lowlands know. There is a beast. There is something that comes in the night.

**Slim**
Well, you're gonna have to handle him alone then, 'cause me and Shadow is hightailin' it outa' here. Shadow! Shadow! Get up, boy!

> SLIM *goes to* SHADOW *and shakes him.* SHADOW *jumps up as though wakened out of a sound sleep.*

**Shadow**

I'm gonna need some new tread on that left rear. Don't wanna make no pit stops the first time around.

**Slim**

Shadow! Listen to me! We been fooled! We been taken for a couple dumb ranch hands. There ain't no beast at all. You was right all along.

> SHADOW *gets up and begins to move about the stage as though preparing for a stock car race.*

**Maria**

He very sick.

**Shadow**

Just make sure the windows is busted out. I don't want to be stickin' my head through no glass. Where's my gloves? I need my gloves!

**Gris Gris**

Gloves coming up.

> GRIS GRIS *goes to* SHADOW *and puts a pair of invisible gloves on his hands.*

**Slim**

You stay away from him. You done enough damage already.

**Preacher**

If you think I'm evil, evil is what I am. A poacher by trade. A preacher poacher. At night my skiff skims the surface of the bayou swamp. Slides noiseless down through lily pads. Bullfrogs jump out of my path.

> *He sheds the skin of the* PREACHER.

**Shadow**

I'll need my helmet too. Just in case. Don't wanna get no whiplash.

**Gris Gris**

Helmet!

**Slim**

Shadow!

**Preacher**

We boys, we young ones ain't been schooled in the morals. A gator's a gator. Long scaly prehistoric, jagged tooth fish beast. With a hide that brings money.

**Shadow**

My dark glasses! My shades! My ankles need to be taped.

**Slim**

What you done to him? What you done to my boy?

**Shadow**

Check the crank case! Transmission! Four forward! On the floor! Radiator! Fan belt! Tachometer set! Rip off them mud flaps, we ain't gonna be in no slush! This is asphalt country!

**Preacher**

At night we go shinin'. Flashlights like little ember fires glazing along the surface. Catch the gleam of the gator's eyes. Like two big cigars burning in the night. A twenty-two short 'll do the trick.

**Slim**

You take that curse off him!

**Gris Gris**

He's not cursed. He's saved. Look at his eyes. He's in heaven driving flat out through the pearlie gates!

**Shadow**

Take the first bank at a hundred and twenty. Push the straight away up to one eighty. Back it down! Down shift! Keep it outa' fourth! Slipstream the Corvettes! Watch out for the red Pontiac! Number seven! Number seven! Break him out of the chute! Now!

**Gris Gris**

Now! Go to it, cowboy!

> SHADOW *sits down on the floor and pretends he's behind the wheel of a stock car. He goes through the sounds and actions of shifting and driving in a full tilt race to the death.*

**Slim**

Maria! Would you stop that mumbling! We gotta get some order in this house! Maria!

**Preacher**

Some boys like to rope and wrestle 'em. But not us. We like to be cruel. Shoot 'em right between the eyes.

They die right on the soot and turn over on their back-
sides, and float right to the surface.

**Slim**

All right! Cut out all this nonsense or I'm gonna start
whippin' some ass!

**Preacher**

Then you drag 'em up on shore. Jamie Lee has his
hatchet out and turns the gator over. He chops straight
down into the neck. The legs jump out and twitch like
a giant frog.

**Slim**

Girl, you undo your black spell or I'm gonna plug ya'
right here and now. This has gone far enough. You got
everybody off the deep end here.

**Gris Gris**

You gonna plug me, gunman? You gonna shoot me
down with your six gun? You gonna make me believe
you got power in your hands? You got no power. Look
around ya'. Look where the power lies. You can't even
pull a nickel outa' yer blue jeans, let alone a pistol.

**Slim**

Now don't push me, gal. I'm about at the end of my
tether.

**Gris Gris**

Oh yeah, you a mean hombre. I can tell by your outfit.

**Maria**

The saints bleed! And all around we are blind! We are
blind to the sun! Blind to the moon and stars!

**Preacher**

Then me, I use my knife. Cut a clean line from the
throat all the way down to the tail. We flop him back over
on his belly and peel away that skin like a new suit a'
clothes. It comes off clean with a little tugging.

**Slim**

You don't know what it takes, girl. One twitch of the
mind. One little snap of the head and I can turn you
into a prairie dog, a varmint, a critter low enough to

blast into dust. It don't take nothin' but a moment! All I gotta do is decide. And if I make that choice, you bein' a female ain't gonna save your hide.

**Gris Gris**

Well, come on then! What's holdin' you back? You can see the worst is comin'. You can see the worst is here knockin' at the door. What do you got to lose?

**Slim**

I'm warnin' you!

**Preacher**

Sometimes we gotta use the pliers to get a good grip. And then we roll the skin up into a little package for the buyers and stick it deep down in a gunny sack. Nothin' left in the mud but a pink naked corpse with the blood oozing down into the earth.

**Gris Gris**

Now fight that corpse, boy! You gotta fight that corpse! There's some life left in him yet.

> The PREACHER *begins to wrestle an imaginary alligator. He writhes and moans all over the stage.*

**Slim**

I'm warnin' you! A killer ain't a pretty sight. I done it before and I'll do it again! I've seen 'em with prayers in their eyes. I've seen 'em with wife and kids cowering in the corner. I've seen 'em bold and ready to die. All kinds. And they was all the same. At that moment they was all the same. Just like you standin' there, arms open, ready for the bullet. It's just a simple thing. Just a simple little thing.

**Gris Gris**

Come on, cowboy man! Come on!

> She plays her fiddle and dances, daring him to kill her.

**Slim**

But I ain't the same. Something's changed. It used to be like makin' love in the highest form. I felt clean and free after it was done. I felt cleansed by the hands of Jesus himself. I felt a flashing burn go up my spine and down the inside of my legs. They fell. They all fell. Oh, the power in that moment! If I could only have that power again! That incredible power to kill and not be afraid. If I could only get it back!

**Gris Gris**
It's here! Here it is! Here I am!

**Slim**
To slaughter a lamb ain't the same.

**Gris Gris**
How 'bout a bird? An eagle or a crow! I can be what you make me. I can turn into a fawn. A white buffalo. An antelope! A wolf! Make me what you want!

**Slim**
It's gone! It's gone, I tell ya'!

> MARIA *rises and crosses down stage, a bright yellow spot on her.*

**Maria**
And a great portent appeared in heaven, a woman clothed with the sun, with the moon under her feet and on her head a crown of twelve stars; she was with child and she cried out in her pangs of birth, in anguish for delivery.

**Slim**
Everything's broken like glass. The time's gone. The past. The blood's gone from my hands. I'm frozen like a rock. Ancient. Nothing moves. I don't feel a thing.

> GRIS GRIS *wails on her fiddle.* SHADOW, *the* PREACHER *and* MARIA *keep up their rituals.* SLIM *staggers around like a madman trying to find himself.*

I move outside myself. It must have been another time. That's it! Another time! This is wrong! I'm not here at all. It was honky tonks and bathtub gin! Railroad men and mule skinners! That was it! This is all wrong! I'm out of my depth. The hands reach for something else now! There's a different craving! A new hunger! I'm starving to death and fat on buffalo meat! What is it a man cries for when nothing fits? No sense to the music? A new kind of music! A new kind of dance!

**Maria**

And another portent appeared in heaven; behold a great red dragon with seven heads and ten horns and seven diadems upon his head. His tail swept down a third of the stars of heaven and cast them to the earth. And the dragon stood before the woman who was about to bear a child, that he might devour her child when she brought it forth; she brought forth a male child, one who was to rule all the nations with a rod of iron, but her child was caught up to God and to his throne and the woman fled into the wilderness where she has a place prepared by God.

**Preacher**

Ya' just tickle his belly. It's the simplest thing. He turns into a puppy dog before your very eyes.

> *Suddenly the door crashes in and the beast enters. He is just as MARIA described. Two heads like a pig, he snorts and spits; lights come from his eyes. His skin is covered with slimy green moss. All the characters continue their rituals, oblivious of the beast's presence. The beast crosses downstage center and faces the audience. The action happens around him. Somehow the beast seems helpless and alone in the situation. He exits.*

**Slim**

Something's taking me over! A scavenger! A coyote dog!

> *GRIS GRIS starts hooting like an owl and playing her fiddle. She begins to take on the fluttering movements of the owl. The PREACHER becomes the alligator. He slithers across the floor and attacks SHADOW, chomping down on him. SHADOW becomes a bull, snorting and pawing at the ground, trying to gore the alligator with his horns. MARIA becomes a wildcat, screaming and prowling around the stage. They each have their own animal rhythms and play them out against each other. SLIM transforms into a coyote, howling at the moon. This happens slowly as he says his monologue. "Jilala" is heard softly in the background. It rises slowly*

*through the scene and becomes deafening by the end of the play.*

You can't take me now! I ain't had my day! I mean I did! I did! But it ain't over! This can't be what I'm left with! Not now! I'll practice up! Just wait! Wait and see! I'll get it back! I'll get back the touch! I got some magic left! I'll take a little vacation! How's that sound? Go up in the hills and practice. Yeah. I could do that. No harm in a little rest. Won't take no jobs for a month. Maybe a year. Sure. A nice long rest. Get my nerves back.

*He howls.*

Just give me a chance! I got both my feet on the ground. I ain't a man a' God! I love the earth! I love the land! This is me talking! Just listen for a little bit longer. Just a little bit. Don't take me without a word. I know you suffer. I can see your silhouette. I feel your pain. You don't have to prove it. I'm your man. It's no mistake. But let me say my piece. Just let me speak it out.

*He howls again.*

That's your voice. I've heard it in the West. I've heard it yapping around my campfires. But you never listened to me! You never did! Don't you think it's fair?

SLIM *drops to his knees and begins to take on the soul of the coyote as he talks. He starts to move around the stage on all fours.*

I'm beyond prayers now! Can't you see that? I never chose my moves. Something moved in me like a silent hand. Every action, every thought. You can take me now! It's all right. Now you can have me! Come on, you old desert dog! Come on! I howl!

*He howls.*

I yap!

*He yaps.*

I chew on the carcass of a skunk. I trot across highways where no cars come for days. I devour my young. I am the beast. The beast is me. I'm feeling your blood now.

It's thinner. Your heart beats faster. You look to the right and the left with quick jerks. Afraid to be eaten yourself. Small animals crawl through your skin. You're infected with desert life. Your loneliness is beyond what humans know. You've given yourself to the ground and I give myself to you. It's only fair. It's only fair.

> SLIM *howls and turns into the coyote. The whole stage is animated with the animal movements and sounds of the characters. The music rises to its highest pitch, then everything goes to silence.*

### BLACKOUT

### THE END

# Shaved Splits

SHAVED SPLITS was first produced at Cafe LaMama on July 20, 1970. The cast:

*Cherry* ......................... Madelaine Leroux
*Wong* ................................ Ching Yeh
*Geez* ............................... Lee Kissman
*Masseuse* ........................ Victor Eschbach

Directed by Bill Hart; lights, Johnny Dodd; sound, Charles Mingus III.

# Scene:

*The bedroom chambers of the Castle Cherry. Everything is pink and puffy. The walls and floors are covered with pink fuzz. The whole ceiling is a mirror, also the upstage wall. Other full-length mirrors in different places. A round window stage right. Center stage is a large oval pink puffy bed with white fuzzy pillows. MISS CHERRY, a young redhead, lies voluptuously on the bed in a pink negligee with nothing underneath, puffy white slippers, a box of chocolates nearby, a radio and color T.V. also in easy reach. The T.V. is on with no sound. Stacked all around the bed and on it are dozens of paperback pornography books. CHERRY is reading one on her back, gobbling chocolates and twisting voluptuously into different suggestive poses. The lights are black. CHERRY'S VOICE is heard reading sexily to herself over the P.A. in the dark. The lights fade up as the VOICE continues. She moves around as she reads.*

**Cherry's Voice**

His mighty cock glistened in the half white light of the moon. It seemed to stand on its own, as though miraculously separated from the man, the boy. The lips of Cherry's moist cunt throbbed with the anticipation of its entry. Slowly, painfully, she eased herself down onto the rough edges where he had been circumcized and then back up again so that the tip almost came completely out. The sinewy hands gripped her breasts and the thumbs ran circles of ecstasy around her erect nipples. Her long back arched like a bow letting her incredibly long red hair fall between his thighs. Suddenly his magnificent member rose and plunged deep between her legs. Tiny electric shocks of joy splintered across her buttocks as she felt his long shaft fill her completely. She ached to have him draw it back down across her clitoris but he held it firm as though testing her endurance. Cherry's lips parted in a half smile as the great prick throbbed in her vagina. She wondered about this boy as she gazed down at the shock of long blonde hair, almost as long as hers. Obviously he was no sissy. He could wield his tool better than almost any she'd had. Except for Darren. Maybe. She was trying to compare in her memory as the boy's cock held firm and steady. Maybe he was holding so still because he was afraid he'd come if he moved. She was trying to remember where she first met him. But then it didn't matter so long as he came once a week to her house. Such a strange young man. He always wore silk and patent leather shoes and batman sunglasses. And always the guitar, the electric guitar which he never played. In fact he never spoke either, a fact which suddenly surprised her. Funny, it never surprised her before. A tinge of fear crossed through her brain but she shook it away. The giant penis began to slide slowly, ever so slowly back out to the opening. Now, she thought, he's going to surprise me. He always does. That was the most exciting part about him. He was never predictable. Suddenly the cock slid all the way out and the boy sat up straight on the pillow, knocking Cherry backwards off the bed. He leapt off the bed and bent over to pick up his vinyl pants. Cherry was desperate; she hadn't had it for more than a week now. She went to her knees on the floor and grabbed both his thighs. Her mouth searched hungrily for his prick and found it. She lapped it up like a dog licking a pan of milk. Her tongue licked over the smooth tip and down along the crack. She gobbled it down and wanted to swallow it whole. Both her hands reached for the beautiful round testicles hanging freely. She squeezed and ran her fingers along the insides of his thighs, then up the crack in his anus. She grabbed hold of both sides of his buttocks and jammed the cock deeper until it almost went down her throat. Then she could taste the warm juices of the young man's sperm oozing into her throat. But something about it tasted strangely different this time. This time it tasted like urine. It was urine! She spit the prick out and screamed.

> CHERRY *throws the book on the floor.*

**Cherry**
Oh no! That's disgusting!

> *She screams for her manservant.*

Wong! Wong!

> WONG *immediately appears. He is a young Chinese with long black hair and dressed in the costume of his country.*

**Wong**
Yes, Miss Cherry.

**Cherry**
I'm not a "Miss," I'm a "Mrs."

**Wong**
Yes, Mrs. Cherry.

**Cherry**
Tell that creep Chunky Puke not to bring me no more trash or his ass is grass. You got that?

**Wong**
Yes, Miss Cherry.

**Cherry**
This last bunch he brought me is downright filthy.

**Wong**
Yes, Miss Cherry.
**Cherry**
And what's all that commotion been goin' on down on the street? Sounds like a riot or somethin'.
**Wong**
I don't hear, Miss Cherry.
**Cherry**
Well, take the stuffin' outa' your ears. There's been all hell breakin' loose down there for the past hour.
**Wong**
I don't hear.
**Cherry**
Any word from D.T. yet?
**Wong**
No, Miss Cherry.
**Cherry**
Well, get a hot wire off to Paris or somethin'. He's probably fucking around at the damn peace table or something.
**Wong**
Yes, Miss Cherry.
**Cherry**
And don't be so servile all the time. Act like a human being, for Christ's sake. You are a human being, aren't you?
**Wong**
Yes, Miss Cherry.
**Cherry**
Then act like one! You don't see me resting on no laurels, do you? Or putting on airs? I could, you know. I got plenty to put on airs about. I got as much to put on airs about as those damn bitch cunts on the Riviera. More maybe. I got a rich influential husband, plenty of money, a yacht, no, two yachts, a Jaguar XKE, an Alfa Romeo, a Mini Cooper, a Fiat Abarth, a Ford Cobra and a lot of other stuff. What's that fucking noise!
*She jumps out of bed and goes to the window.*

**Wong**

Nothing, Miss Cherry.

**Cherry**

Oh nothing my ass, you dumb chink. There's something going on down there and I know it. You probably know it too. Don't you?

> *She turns on* WONG *and slinks toward him.*

You wouldn't be holding out on me now, would you? Cherry likes to know if there's a party going on.

**Wong**

Nothing, Miss Cherry.

**Cherry**

I'll bet you have a really nice Wong, don't you, Wong.

> *She grabs* WONG *by the balls. He pulls away.*

O.K., Chinaman. Get the fuck out! Get out!

> WONG *exits.*

Time was when no man would turn me down. No man! Fucking D.T. hired a bunch a' faggot servants, that's for sure. How's a Cherry supposed to get her rocks off in this pink fuzzy womb. Fuckin' place is one big faggoty armpit. Fuckin' D.T.'s probably a faggot. That's probably how come he hired a bunch of faggots. Sure. It all makes sense. Everything fits together. I'm probably a fucking front for his fucking faggotry. He takes me out once in a while to show everyone he's not a faggot, when all the time he really is one. I've been used! That's how come he never comes home. That's how come he hasn't been home for six weeks. He's out there sucking on some faggot's joint and probably getting it up the ass by another faggot. He's probably on some faggot dude ranch in Arizona or something. Fucking faggot!

> *Gunfire is heard coming from the street below.* CHERRY *goes to the window again and opens it. She yells out the window.*

America! Love it or leave it, motherfuckers!

> *She closes the window again.*

That's all I need is an insurrection. Right now. That's really what I need. Stuck in some stupid fairy's castle in the middle of a goddamn revolution. Neato jet. Super keen. Out a' sight. Far fucking out.

*A knock on the door.*

Yeah!

*A VOICE with a French accent from outside.*

**Voice**

It ees time for your French lesson, Miss Cherry.

**Cherry**

Go fuck yourself in the mouth! What the fuck am I gonna do with a French lesson? Seen any Frenchmen lately? Tell that big bruiser—what's his name—to come up here. The masseuse. What's his name?

**Voice**

Masseuse, mademoiselle.

**Cherry**

Yeah. Masseuse. Tell him to get his ass up here. I need a rubdown.

*She goes to the bed and flops on it.*

Everybody's a servant around here. Nothing but fucking servants and faggots.

*She opens another book and reads it.*
*Her voice is heard over the P.A.*

**Cherry's Voice**

This time it looked like curtains for the dynamic duo. There they were, cornered on one side by the evil Mikon and about to be swallowed whole by the Mikon's giant python which slithered lengthwise over the shining marble floor straight for the . . .

**Cherry**

Who gives a rat's ass!

*She throws the book down and picks up another one. The VOICE again.*

**Cherry's Voice**

There he lay in the red clay with his belly ripped open and the guts pouring down both his legs. It took everything he had to grab the intestines with both hands and shove his insides back in his stomach. Already he noticed the black vultures circling hungrily, just biding their time.

Somewhere in the back of his brain he knew he would survive. He had to. Just to live long enough to get back to Alvarez and gun down that son of a bitch Garringa.

> MASSEUSE *enters. He is huge and muscular, shaved head, no shirt and Russian type pants with black boots.*

**Cherry**
It's about fucking time. Come on. You can really sock it to me today. I ache all over.

> *She lies on her stomach.* MASSEUSE *goes to her and starts massaging her back.*

I'm gonna get you to talk today if it kills me. You savvy, Masseuse. You're gonna speak to me today. It's not right, being able to put your filthy hands all over my body and never speaking a word. Who knows what's going on in that brain of yours. You could be fantasizing all kinds of dirty things. Unless you're a faggot too. Are you, Masseuse? Are you a faggot in disguise? You could have fooled me. It's not natural for a man to be feeling me up and not even think about sticking it in. Do you want to put it in me, Masseuse? If you tell me, then I could at least think about it. What do you say? You wanna slide your big thing between my legs? I'll bet you'd love that, wouldn't you? Ouch! Watch it, you clown! I'm not a piece of goddamn meat. You must have to get pretty weird in the head to do a job like yours. I mean dig yourself. As far as you're concerned I'm not even a person. Just a body, a hunk of flesh for you to squeeze and manhandle. How do you get your kicks anyway. Dirty pictures? I bet you masturbate over the bra ads in the *Sunday Times* magazine section. You don't have to be shy, Masseuse. We all have our little idiosyncrasies. There's a war down there in the streets, you know. Really. What do you think about revolution, Masseuse? Personally, I think it's a waste of time. Just a stupid exchange of power. A plot to make the rich poor and the poor stay poor. What do you think? Do you have any opinions at all, you big jerk? Do you think thoughts? I guess not. They say the lower classes are happier even though they're lower. What do you think about that one? I mean it's a possibility. Since you don't think thoughts, then you can't very well get depressed, can you? Depression comes from thinking, don't you think? Thinking negative. Elation comes from thinking positive. Happiness comes from not thinking at all. How 'bout that logic. Do it lower. Lower! That's it. Good boy. I mean you can't separate thinking and feeling, they're two sides to the same coin. Interdependent. Right? For example, I could suddenly get a tinge of joy and then wham, a whole flood of positive thoughts comes gushing into my brain. In that case my emotions or my soma acts on my psyche. It also works in reverse, like I said before. You think a happy thought and then you feel happy. The psyche acts on the soma. We're victims of paradox, Masseuse. Up and down, up and down, up and down. But what about a system of existence where it works side-ways? In other words you cut straight across all that mind fuck business, depression, elation, manic-depresso and find yourself in a steady flowing stream of cool clear water. You see what I'm getting at. Instead of looking at being alive as an up and down struggle on a vertical scale of profit and loss, win and lose, add and subtract like those assholes on the street out there, you begin to see it as a whole piece that includes that other stuff, but it works horizontally instead. Do you get my meaning? I should write a goddamn book. Higher! That's it. That's good. They're not lover's hands, but they'll do. You know what's going to happen to you if that commotion down there gets out of hand? If the underdogs win? You'll be out of a job. How's that grab you? Same thing happened during the Civil War in the name of "emancipating the nigger." Hundreds of niggers wandering around home-less, starving to death, singing the blues. When before the war started they had a nice home, three squares and some spare change in their pockets. Now it's happening all over again. This is a fucked up country. You know that,

Masseuse? A schizophrenic country. Split right up the middle. It's never gotten together and it never will. Thing is you gotta make sense out of all the chaos or else you're up shit creek. Right? You gotta make yourself a personal world where things work the way they're supposed to. Where you're comfy and warm.

> WONG *enters.*

**Wong**
Miss Cherry.

**Cherry**
Yeah?

**Wong**
Mr. Chunky Puke is here to see you.

**Cherry**
Tell him to sit on his thumb.

**Wong**
Yes, Miss Cherry.

**Cherry**
No, tell him to come in here. I have a thing or two to say to that creep.

**Wong**
> *To offstage.*

Miss Cherry see you now.

> CHUNKY PUKE *enters. He is a short, fat, ugly little man with wraparound sunglasses, baseball cap, a long funky gray overcoat with patches all over it and black tennis shoes. He carries a big briefcase.* MASSEUSE *keeps working on* CHERRY'S *back.*

**Chunky Puke**
Hi ya', sister. How's tricks?

**Cherry**
Come over here, you meatball.

> *He crosses to the bed and sets his briefcase on it.*

**Chunky Puke**
What're you in the mood for today?

> *He opens the briefcase and starts taking out paperback porno books and handing them to* CHERRY. *She reads the titles.*

**Cherry**

None of that garbage you brought me last time. That last batch was downright disgusting. And I'm pretty broad-minded.

**Chunky Puke**

How 'bout a little lesbian tickler?

> *He hands her a book.*

**Cherry**

> *Reading the title.*

"Leatherbound Lezzies." Terrific.

**Chunky Puke**

I got some nice sado-masochism here. How 'bout that? Good for a nightcap.

**Cherry**

"Whiplash Hermaphrodites."

**Chunky Puke**

Here's the latest from Italy.

**Cherry**

"Six Virgin Nuns Ravaged by Africans."

> *He keeps handing her books and she reads the titles. The briefcase should be much smaller than the amount of books that come out of it. This could be done with a false bottom and a hole in the bed where the books come from, as in the circus.*

"Bluff at Coyote Ridge." "Sheba Meets the Warlock." "Shameful Charlatan." "Ordeal at Sesame Creek." "Virgo and the Virgin." "Rape on Times Square." "Lampooned for Lust." "Slaughter at Dust Bowl Springs." "The Truth Behind the Myth of the Hell's Angels." "The Sweet Scent of Love." "Martian Matron." "Horny in Vietnam." "The Castrated Male in American Society." "Wicked Wanderer." "Dago's in Drag." "Bon Bon Beauty." "Cheeseburger Hard On." "Bitch Goddess." "Surfer Queen and Her Fantastic Machine." "Custer's Last Stand." "Chopped and Channeled." "Star Ship War Lord." "Last Chance for Chastity." "Cream of the Crop." "Plastic Orgiastic." "Sex Among the Zulu." "Sin Servants." "The Stiletto and the

Stud." "Milk Maid." "War Among the Cryptoids." "Razors in the Rumbleseat." "Backwoods Scandal." "Honeysuckle Suckling." "Hungry Handsome." "The Visit of the Moist Wet Terror." "Funky Faggot." "Dirty Deal on Fantasy Mountain." "Frontier Phantom." "Boogie Bitch." "How L.S.D. Sent Me to the Gas Chamber." "Kiss of the White Witch." "More Tales of Lust and Passion by Herman Hype." "The Secret Sex Life of Mick Jagger." "Sordid Solo." "The Confessions of B. Mitchell Reed." "Juicy Jet Set." "The Mangled Morbid." "Annette Funicello Tells All." "Hashish Assassins." "Syncopated Shimmy." "Sing Out with the Kingston Trio." "Hypos and Pimps." "Satisfying Sunday." "Big Red Meat." "Mojo Man." "Hungover Hipster." "Bad Ass Bikey." "Bad Day at Black Rock." "Monkey in the Works." "Betty Grable's Last Regret." "The History of Cassius Clay." "Miscarriage." "The Man Behind the Lovely Lennon Sisters." "I Slept with Al Capone." "What Ringo Starr Won't Tell His Mother." "Double Entendre." "Ukrainian Fairy Tales." "The Treasure of Quetzalcoatl." "Riverboat Rape." "Berkeley Bombshell." "Minnesota Fats Meets the Tambourine Man." "The Changing Climate of the American University." "How Rock and Roll Robbed My Children." "What the Bayou Girls Don't Know." "Schizo-Frantic." "Sex Crazed Gypsy." "The Return of the Salamander." "Beaver Layout." "Wall of White Flesh." "Junkie on a Jag." "Hot Rod Hooker." "The Naughty Lady of Shady Lane." "Lazy Lay." "Fever in the Pockets." "Borscht Belt Broad." "Paranoia Killed the Cat." "Strange Bedfellows." "The Werewolf's Revenge." "Demon in Blue Jeans." "Hippie Harlots."

Not bad. I'll take 'em all.
**Chunky Puke**
I figured you'd go for this batch.
**Cherry**
It's not that they're so terrific. I'm just bored. You know. Today I'm feeling particularly bored.

**Chunky Puke**

I know how ya' feel, sweetheart. I get that way myself sometimes.

**Cherry**

Do you really? And I'll bet you just sit on the can and gobble these things up, don't you?

**Chunky Puke**

I sell 'em, I don't read 'em.

**Cherry**

Well, that's a good practice, Mr. Puke. You can get your money from Wong. Now get out of here.

**Chunky Puke**

O.K., sister. Enjoy yourself now. Don't buy any wooden nickels.

**Cherry**

Scram!

> CHUNKY PUKE *exits with his bag.*

You can split too, Gabby. Go on! Get your paws off me and beat it!

> MASSEUSE *exits.*

God! Why hast thou forsaken me.

> *She picks up a book and starts to read. Her voice comes over the P.A.*

**Cherry's Voice**

Cherry was at her wits' end. It had been more than a week since the young man with the vinyl pants had rung her doorbell. She was beginning to panic. Could she be that unappealing? She gazed at her gaunt face with the high cheekbones and moistened her lips. No. She was too ravishing. No man could turn her down. She opened her blouse and let the fine oval milk-white breasts unfold before the mirror. She ran her long nails over the nipples and closed her eyes, half smiling to herself. Her left hand gently massaged its way down her rib cage and nestled between her thighs. She teased herself softly and imagined the face of the boy, tense and arrogant, yet somehow tender and loving at the same time. Her buttocks shivered with the thought of his prick. So firm and smooth, so savage. His warrior-like back, the sinewy muscles of his thighs and calves, the hands. His hands were something special. Perhaps it was because he played the guitar. The way the veins stood out on his thumbs and bulged into his wrists like rushing rivers charging toward the ocean. The pale blue eyes which seemed like an ancient Aztec painting and a grammar school boy all at once. How strange that they knew each other only once a week. How strange they should live in two different worlds. So completely strangers.

> GEEZ, *a young revolutionary, bursts into the room. He walks with a limp. He is very shaggy and dirty. Long hair and beard with an earring and a bloody bandage around his head. He wears a pea green army fatigue jacket with two straps of ammunition criss-crossing from shoulder to waist. An M-1 rifle, a pistol on his hip. Faded muddy blue jeans and old cowboy boots. CHERRY gasps and reaches for the telephone.*

**Geez**

Forget it. It's been chopped off. Just stay put.

> *He aims the rifle at her, then goes to the oval window and opens it.*

Nice aquarium you got here.

**Cherry**

Listen, Daddyo . . .

**Geez**

No, you listen! Just keep your mouth shut, sexy.

> *He looks out the window again, then turns back into the room. He takes off the ammunition belt and unbuttons his jacket. He sits on the floor and rolls the pantleg up on his wounded leg.*

**Cherry**

Want me to get you some medicine?

**Geez**

I want you to do like I told you.

**Cherry**

I know, but you're hurt.

**Geez**
And you're gonna help me, right. You're gonna bop down to the local pharmacy in your negligee and cop me some nice drugs for the pain.

**Cherry**
No.

**Geez**
No. You're gonna run to the nearest doctor and tell him there's a bearded freak bleeding to death in your boudoir. Won't he please come and bring his little black bag.

**Cherry**
I was going to ...

**Geez**
Shut up! Just shut up and sit tight.

**Cherry**
Then there really is a war going on down there?

**Geez**
Just a little misunderstanding. It'll be all better in the morning. How many doors you got in this place?

**Cherry**
I don't know.

**Geez**
Take a guess.

**Cherry**
Thirty-five or forty. Maybe fifty.

**Geez**
And there's only one way into this room?

**Cherry**
Yeah. Why?

> GEEZ *gets up and goes to the bed.*

**Geez**
Get up.

**Cherry**
Why? What're you going to do to me?

> GEEZ *grabs* CHERRY *and throws her off the bed. He rips the fuzzy pink blanket off the bed. All the books crash to the floor.*

What the fuck are you doing?

> GEEZ *takes the blanket and goes to the door. He bolts the door shut and starts ripping the blanket up.*

Hey! Cut it out! That came all the way from Paris, France.

**Geez**

No shit. I came all the way from East L.A. and they're still ripping me up.

> *He starts stuffing the blanket in between the cracks in the door.*

**Cherry**

What's that for? You're going to cut off all the air! Hey look, buster, if you plan to commit suicide why don't you let me go. I didn't do anything to you.

**Geez**

You ever heard of tear gas?

**Cherry**

I've read about it in the *New York Times.*

**Geez**

Good. Then you know all there is to know.

> *He hobbles to the bed and sits on it, rolling his pantleg up again.*

**Cherry**

What do you mean? Are you trying to tell me they're going to tear gas my castle? Are they? Wong! Wong!

**Geez**

He's locked up, lady.

**Cherry**

Look, there's no reason to keep me here. I won't tell anyone you're here if you just let me go. I promise.

**Geez**

Cross your heart and hope to die?

> CHERRY *runs for the door.* GEEZ *points the rifle at her.*

I've killed about fourteen people today. At first it was a little traumatic. Put me through a lot of changes. But now I know I can do it. Any time, anywhere. Now you better believe that, lady.

**Cherry**

You don't scare me.

**Geez**

Good. Maybe we'll get along famously. Now the first thing I need is some food. You got any food?

**Cherry**

Down in the kitchen. I'll just go down . . .

**Geez**

Get it straight. We're stuck here, you and me, for as long as it takes me to make my next move. That window's a good sniping spot. You can see the whole street.

**Cherry**

Don't tell me you're going to start shooting that gun in here. You'll get us all killed.

**Geez**

Us? How many of *us* are there?

**Cherry**

Well, there's me and you and all the servants.

**Geez**

How many servants?

**Cherry**

There's Wong and Masseuse and Francoise and the Chef and the kitchen help and the maid and . . .

**Geez**

That's enough.

**Cherry**

But they're liable to go to the cops. You'd better go down and lock them up or something.

**Geez**

They've been liberated, lady. All except for Wong or whatever his name is. He wanted to be loyal. What about your old man? Do you have an old man?

**Cherry**

My father? Leave my father out of this.

**Geez**

Your hubby, honey. Your love man.

**Cherry**

D.T.? He's gone.

**Geez**

When's he due back?

**Cherry**

I don't know. I haven't heard from him in six weeks.

**Geez**

You must be horny then.

**Cherry**

Don't get smart.

**Geez**

Oh boy, chocolate delights.

*He grabs the box of chocolates and gobbles them.*

**Cherry**

Are you a student?

**Geez**

Do I look like one?

**Cherry**

I'm just trying to be civil. It seems that if we're forced to be with each other we might as well be polite.

**Geez**

By all means. The first rule of thumb when two people are caught up together in the middle of an insurrection is that they should be polite. If it wouldn't be too much trouble would you please pass me the blood plasma and the tourniquet before my leg falls off.

**Cherry**

O.K., wise guy. Could I at least have my bed back?

**Geez**

Are you wounded or something?

**Cherry**

I'm a woman and that's my bed.

**Geez**

You're a dumb cunt and this bed is liberated territory! In fact everywhere I walk, sit, stand or lie down is liberated territory. That means you're welcome to come sit on it if you want to. It's a free bed. But don't tell me it's yours and not mine because I'll burn it to the ground and then it won't even be there to argue about.

**Cherry**

Just be careful with that gun. You can do whatever you want but just watch that gun.

**Geez**

Are you afraid of guns?

**Cherry**

Yes, as a matter of fact, I am. They give me the creeps.

**Geez**

But people are what make guns work. I make this one work. I'm personally responsible for when this rifle goes off and when it doesn't. Whoever falls in front of this rifle falls because of me, not the rifle. Free choice, you dig?

**Cherry**

I dig.

**Geez**

But you said you weren't afraid of me, so why should you be afraid of my piece? If you're afraid of it accidentally going off, don't be. I don't make mistakes.

**Cherry**

I wish I could say that makes me feel better.

**Geez**

You don't have to trust me if you don't want to.

**Cherry**

Do I have a choice?

**Geez**

Yeah. Mistrust me.

**Cherry**

I think it's better if we just don't talk.

> *She moves toward the window.*

**Geez**

It depends. It can be lonely both ways. Stay away from that window.

**Cherry**

Why? Do you think I'm going to signal or something?

**Geez**

The man is down there and as soon as he figures out that I'm up here he's going to start shooting at anything that moves past that window.

**Cherry**

This is great! Trapped on one side by a freaked-out revolutionary type and on the other by our boys in blue. And right in my own home too. I didn't even have to go out looking for trouble, it came to me.

**Geez**

It's better than T.V., you'll have to admit. No pauses for those irksome commercials. No static. No greasy politicians. No late late Bela Lugosi movies.

**Cherry**

I happen to like Bela Lugosi.

**Geez**

Why? What did he ever do for you? Did you know that in real life he lured young chicks up to his castle in the Hollywood Hills and tortured them?

**Cherry**

Sure.

**Geez**

It's true. And so did Erich von Stroheim. Cigarette butts on the tits and stuff. Real nasty.

*A police bullhorn comes bellowing from the street.*

**Bullhorn**

All right, Geez! We know you're in there! Throw out your weapons and give yourself up! This is the police! You've had fair warning!

*GEEZ leaps off the bed and rushes to the window. He throws it open and yells out.*

**Geez**

And this is me, motherfucker! If you want me, come up and get me, you stupid pig bastard faggots!

*He points the rifle out the window and fires. Rapid return fire is heard from the street. GEEZ ducks back inside. CHERRY rushes for the door and tries to unlock it.*

Get away from that door or I'll kill you!

*CHERRY freezes.*

Now I told you about that before. You and me are here to stay.

**Cherry**

What'd you have to go and yell at them for? They wouldn't have even known you were here.

**Geez**

I want them to know. I want them to know it's not going to be easy.

**Cherry**

Aren't you afraid?

**Geez**

No.

**Cherry**

To die, I mean.

**Geez**

Look at this leg. I'm dying already. I just hope they come up here before it's all over.

*He limps over to the bed and flops on it.*

**Cherry**

Well, aren't you the brave hero. If you had any sense you would have rested up here, gotten something to eat and then ducked out the back.

**Geez**

Wong's pretty loyal to you, isn't he?

**Cherry**

I guess so. Why?

**Geez**

Here's what I'm gonna do. I'm gonna open the door and I want you to yell down to him for some food.

**Cherry**

But you said he was locked up.

**Geez**

Shut up. He's in the closet right at the foot of the stairs. He'll be able to hear you. Then I'm gonna go down and un-lock him. Now I want you to just cool it. I'll be right at the foot of the stairs so don't try anything. O.K.?

**Cherry**

O.K. But what difference does it make if I escape? The cops already know you're here.

**Geez**

You're my hostage, lady.

**Cherry**

Oh.

**Geez**
Now come on.
> GEEZ *gets up and goes to the door and opens it.*

**Cherry**
What do you want? Chateau Briand? Vizzis Suas? Crep Sousettes?

**Geez**
You got any bacon and eggs?

**Cherry**
Sure, bacon and eggs coming up. Wong!
> *She yells out the door.*

**Wong's Muffled Voice**
Miss Cherry!

**Cherry**
Listen, Wong. That big guy who came in here, the one who locked you up in the closet? Well, he's a friend of mine. He's real hungry and he wants something to eat. Could you tell the chef . . .

**Geez**
The chef's gone.

**Cherry**
Wong. Do you think you could cook up some ham and eggs . . .

**Geez**
And a glass of milk.

**Cherry**
And a glass of milk!

**Geez**
And some bread.

**Cherry**
And some bread!

**Geez**
And a coffee.

**Cherry**
And a pot of coffee! Do you think you could do that, Wong?

**Voice of Wong**
Yes, Miss Cherry!

**Cherry**

All right. He's coming down to let you out! Now don't be afraid. Just do what I told you. O.K?

**Wong**

Yes, Miss Cherry!

**Geez**

Now get back over on the bed. Go on!

> CHERRY *goes to the bed and sits.*

Now, remember, I'm right at the foot of the stairs, so be cool.

**Cherry**

Don't worry. I'm not going anywhere.

> GEEZ *backs out the door and disappears.* CHERRY *sits tensely for a moment staring at the door, then looking at the window and back to the door again. Suddenly she leaps up and runs for the window screaming for help and waving her arms.*

Help! Police! Help! Up here! Help! Help!

> *Loud rapid gunfire from outside.* CHERRY *is blasted back onto the bed screaming in pain. Her face and neck are all bloody. She clutches her face and writhes on the bed in agony.*

Oh my God! Oh no! I've been shot! I've been shot! They shot me! Oh God! They shot me! They shot me! They shot me!

> *She keeps screaming the same thing over and over until* GEEZ *comes charging back into the room. He goes to* CHERRY *and tries to pull her hands away from her face. He rushes back to the door and bolts it. He goes to the window and looks out. Then back to* CHERRY. CHERRY *is hysterical, screaming and kicking and holding her face.*

**Geez**

Did they get your eyes?

**Cherry**

They shot me! They shot me!

**Geez**

It's bird shot. You'll be all right if they didn't hit your eyes. Let's see. Let me have a look. Come on. It's all right. Let me see.

> *He pries her hands away from her face. Blood is running down her face and neck.*

You'll be all right. Your eyes are still there. Get into bed. Come on. Get under the covers.

> *He helps* CHERRY *under the blankets. She is moaning and holding her face.*

You should a' listened to me. A pig's a pig. He'll kill anything that moves.

**Cherry**

My face! They shot my face! They shot me!

> *A loud knock on the door.* GEEZ *goes to the door with his pistol out.*

**Geez**

Yeah? Wong?

**Wong's Voice**

Yes, Miss Cherry.

> GEEZ *unbolts the door.* WONG *enters with a Chinese dragon mask on his head and traditional ritual costume on. He holds the tray of food over his head and does a weird Balinese type dance, singing in Chinese and moving in weird rhythms.* GEEZ *takes the tray of food and bolts the door again.* WONG *keeps dancing and singing in long slow elongated phrases.* GEEZ *sits on the floor and digs into the food ravenously.* CHERRY *moans and wails.*

**Geez**

Looks like your servant's flipped out, lady.

**Cherry**

Well, you could help me! You could at least help me! I'm bleeding to death!

**Geez**

I was gonna ask Wong here to bring you up some hot water and bandages but it looks like he's too far gone.

> CHERRY *looks at* WONG *still holding her face.*

**Cherry**

Wong! Stop it! What's the matter with you! What's happening! Wong! Tell him to stop it.

**Geez**

Now just stop it, Wong. You're going too far.

**Cherry**

I'm going to go crazy!

**Geez**

Far out. Blow your mind.

**Cherry**

I helped you! I got you some food!

**Geez**

I'm very grateful. As soon as I finish I'll see what I can do.

*Loud gunfire from the street. The* BULLHORN *again.*

**Bullhorn**

Now listen, Geez! This is your last warning! We want you alive but if we have to we'll use force!

*GEEZ goes to the window again and shouts down.*

**Geez**

If you *have* to! You already shot up a woman, you faggots! You cowardly motherfuckers! Come up here and get me if you want me so bad! I'll tear your ass apart! Come on! I'm right here waiting!

*He fires out the window. More return fire.*

**Cherry**

Stop shooting! Stop it! I can't stand it!

**Geez**

Shut up. Go to sleep or something. You're not going to die so stop bellyaching.

*He goes back to his food and digs in.* WONG *keeps flipping out with his dance and singing.*

**Cherry**

Oh I wish I could die! Right now! I wish I was dead!

**Geez**

Wong's really got some beautiful timing, you know. To think he wasted all that serving you. The Orientals have a whole different concept of rhythm from us Occidents. It works on a horizontal line instead of vertical.

**Cherry**

Why can't I die! Oh God! Let me die!

**Geez**

Their theatre's pretty boss too. Every gesture means something, every sound. They tell a whole story with song. Sort of like opera but heavier.

**Cherry**

Just let me die! I don't want to live any more! Let me die!

**Geez**

Die already. Nobody's stopping you. Only you'd be missing out on a whole lot. Those cops are really gonna freak when they walk in here. I wouldn't miss their faces for anything.

**Cherry**

You've got no sympathy at all! You're just like an animal. Worse than an animal!

**Geez**

The same maybe, but no worse.

**Cherry**

Wong! Stop it! What's gotten into you! If you don't stop it I'm going to fire you!

**Geez**

You better cool it, Wong. Your whole livelihood's at stake.

**Cherry**

You're fired!

**Geez**

There! Now you're free, Wong. Finally. You can freak out to your heart's content.

**Cherry**

No! It's not fair! This is my home! My castle!

**Geez**

Just 'cause you knocked up some rich old faggot doesn't give you any claim to ownership.

**Cherry**

Don't you talk about my husband that way.

**Geez**

Why not? *You* probably do when you're alone.

**Cherry**

He's not a faggot. He's a very highly respected man in this country. He's been influential all over the world in helping the poor and the needy and giving to the cancer foundation.

**Geez**

Who gives a rat's ass.

**Cherry**
Don't talk to me that way!

**Geez**
Why not? It's a free country.

**Bullhorn**
All right, Geez! This is your last warning! We're going to start tear gasing in about five minutes. Throw out your guns and come out with your hands over your head.

> *Geez leaps to the window.* WONG *keeps dancing.*

**Geez**
Throw your fucking tear gas! Come on! I'm waiting! And don't give me any more warnings either 'cause I'm warning you! If you don't get your asses up here pretty quick I'm coming down there! And I'm gonna take about six pigs with me when I fall! You got that straight?

> *Gunfire from outside.* GEEZ *goes to the door and stuffs the blanket back in the cracks.*

**Cherry**
I hope they get you. I hope they kill you twice.

**Geez**
They're gonna have to, baby. The way I feel I could take on the whole street. That ham and eggs sure hit the spot. And there's nothing like a little Balinese dancing to give a man inspiration.

> *He whips out a large red bandana from his hip pocket and ties it around his face like a mask.*

You better put your head under the pillow. They're gonna start heaving cannisters through that window any minute.

**Cherry**
Just leave me alone! Don't talk to me.

**Geez**
Poor baby.

**Cherry**
What'd you say?

**Geez**
I said poor baby. Here you thought you were on top of the world and now it turns out you got nothing.

**Cherry**

Don't pity me!

**Geez**

Why not? Nobody else will. I might as well.

**Cherry**

I hate your guts!

> *A smoking tear gas cannister flies in through the window and crashes against a wall. GEEZ rushes to it, picks it up and throws it back out the window. WONG keeps dancing, in another world.*

**Geez**

It's about time! I used to play baseball myself! All American Junior Varsity!

> *He does a mock cheer leader thing out the window to the cops.*

Rah Rah Ree! Kick 'em in the knee! Rah Rah Razz! Kick 'em in the other knee! Fight team fight! Who's gonna win? We're gonna win! Who's gonna lose! They're gonna lose! Push 'em back! Push 'em back! Way back! Push 'em back! Push 'em back! Way back!

> *He dodges gunfire and keeps up the cheering.*

V! V! For Victory! Vah! Vah! For Varsity! Victory for Varsity! Fight team Fight! Gimme a "P"! Gimme an "I"! Gimme a "G"; Gimme a "P," "I," "G"; What does it spell! Pigmeat! Sooee! Sooee! Sooee! Sooee! Sooee! Sooee! Sooee! Sooee!

**Cherry**

Stop it! Stop it! I can't stand it anymore!

> *CHERRY goes into hysteria. The loud sound of a helicopter right above the stage. WONG keeps dancing.*

**Geez**

Ah hah! Trying to get me from above, eh? I'll pop 'em off like flies!

**Cherry**

Don't shoot! That's my husband! That's D.T.!

**Geez**

What? In a helicopter? That's class.

**Cherry**

He's landing on the roof.

**Geez**

I'm hip.

> *The helicopter dies down and gradually stops. The BULL-HORN comes in.*

**Bullhorn**

Hello, the helicopter! Whoever you are don't go in that house! There's a fleeing felon in there!

**Geez**

That's me.

**Voice of D.T.**

> *From roof.*

A what? My wife's in there!

**Bullhorn**

Don't go in there! Stay on the roof and lie flat on your stomach! This is the Police!

**D.T.'s Voice**

This is my home! My wife's in there!

**Bullhorn**

Stay where you are! Don't move!

**D.T.'s Voice**

I've got to see my wife!

**Cherry**

Oh, D.T.! Don't come in here! D.T.!

**Geez**

He loves you. He's coming in here to snatch you from the clutches of a fleeing felon. That's me.

**Cherry**

Don't you hurt him! Don't you dare!

**Geez**

Just stay on the bed!

**Bullhorn**

Geez! There's a civilian about to enter your room! If any harm comes to . . .

> *GEEZ yells out the window.*

**Geez**

You ought to be a newscaster, asshole! I can see what's
going on! I got two eyes and I got two hostages, motherfuckers! Not one but two!

> *Gunfire from outside. Loud knocking on the door. GEEZ
> goes to it and stands on one side.*

**Cherry**

D.T.! No! He'll kill you!

**D.T.'s Voice**

Cherry! Are you all right!

> *More banging. GEEZ unbolts the door and swings it open.
> D.T. rushes in. GEEZ bolts the door shut. D.T. goes to
> CHERRY and holds her. He is an older man, in his late
> fifties. Gray balding head, gray suit and an attache case.*

**D.T.**

Cherry! What's happened to you? Your face. Did you . . .

> *D.T. makes a move for GEEZ. GEEZ holds the rifle on him.
> D.T. stops.*

**Geez**

The little lady got in front of some bird shot. I tried to
warn her but . . .

**D.T.**

> *To* WONG.

Who's this! What's going on here?

**Geez**

This is your servant, Wong, doing a little rendition of "I
Can't Get No Satisfaction."

**D.T.**

Wong! Cherry, what's the meaning of this? I go off on
a little business trip and what do I find when I come back?

**Cherry**

A little business trip! Six weeks! You were gone for six
fucking weeks! Not a letter! Not even a postcard! At least
you could have phoned!

**D.T.**

That's no reason to go off the deep end. Who is this
young man?

**Geez**

She picked me up on Henry Street, sir. I didn't want to come but she was pretty horny.

*D.T. slaps CHERRY across the face.*

**Cherry**

You idiot! Don't believe him! He came charging in here escaping from the cops!

**Geez** .

It's true. I'm a fleeing felon. Glad to meet you.

*He holds his hand out to D.T., who refuses it.*

**D.T.**

Cherry, how do you get yourself into these situations? Last time it was a Puerto Rican conga band.

**Cherry**

Shut up! Get away from me! You're worse than him! Can't you see I've been wounded!

**D.T.**

I'm sorry. Let me get you some water.

*He gets up to go out.*

**Geez**

Nobody's leaving here, pops. Just sit on the bed.

**D.T.**

Of all the nerve. My wife is wounded in the face.

**Geez**

Well, I'm wounded in the heart.

**D.T.**

It doesn't show. What do they want you for?

**Geez**

Manslaughter, armed robbery, inciting to riot, assaulting a police officer, high treason, plotting to overthrow the government of the United States.

**D.T.**

You sure know how to pick them, Cherry.

**Cherry**

I told you, he came charging in here. I never saw him before.

**D.T.**
I suppose there's some sort of exciting titillation in flirting with riff raff. After all they do have that close proximity to death that they carry around like a banner. Waving it in the face of authority. Flaunting it before women as though it were some sign of masculinity and courage.

**Geez**
What have you got to wave, old man? A BankAmericard?

**D.T.**
Their total disregard for the value of a dollar. As though those who know its meaning and struggle for its possession are worse than non-existent.

**Geez**
*To* CHERRY.
Are you going to let him talk to me this way?

**D.T.**
When all the time the shoe in actuality is on the other foot. They see their dilemma. They see it's really they who don't exist, who are threatened with extinction. So they fight the real world with all their vain inane ideology. Hoping against hope that a cause might win over a concrete reality.

**Cherry**
Shut up! You're worse than him.

**D.T.**
The same maybe but no worse. He and I are both wrapped up in a losing struggle against reality.

**Geez**
Speak for yourself, old man.

**D.T.**
I am. The sad part is that we think we can win.

**Geez**
Who's "we," mister? You don't have any "we." All you've got is an "I," a "me." You and all the other "I's" and "me's" out there. That's why you're being shot down right now. Right in your own bedroom. I've got brothers out there on the street. Brothers. "Others." Me and my

brothers are going to eat you and your "I's" up. Call for help, why don't you? Go ahead. Your old lady tried and look at her. Look at her face. What kind of "me" shoots down its own kind? You can't even see you're alone. Your wife knows it. How come you don't?

**D.T.**

Leave my wife out of this.

**Geez**

Up against the wall, motherfucker!

**Cherry**

I know what? What do I know?

**Geez**

That you've been had. Screwed in the ass by your own life. Look at Wong here. You and me can't begin to imagine where he's at. But he's got ahold of something. Look around you. What've you got to fall back on, to trust? You're gonna die in this bedroom and you've got nothing to turn to. Not even each other.

**Cherry**

We're not going to die! We're not going to die! D.T.! Do something!

> *D.T. runs to the window yelling for help and waving his arms.*

**D.T.**

Help! Police! Don't shoot! Don't shoot! Help!

**Geez**

Get away from that window!

**D.T.**

Help! Help! Police! Help! Help!

> *Loud gunfire. D.T. falls back screaming and clutching his shoulder. He falls on the floor. CHERRY stays on the bed. WONG keeps dancing.*

I've been hit! Oh my God! I'm going to die.

**Cherry**

It hurts, doesn't it? Now maybe you'll believe me.

**Geez**

There, see? All those taxes you paid to get shot by the protectors of private property and civil decency.

**D.T.**
I'm dying! I'm dying!
**Geez**
Knock yourself out.
**Cherry**
We're too young to die!
**Geez**
He's not. He's past his prime. Look at him. Fat, bald.
**D.T.**
I'm dying! I'm dying!
> CHERRY *goes to* GEEZ *and falls on her knees to him. D.T. screams over and over.* WONG *dances.*

**Cherry**
Take me with you! Take me! You can have me! All of me.
**Geez**
Who wants all of you? You're too much to handle for one man, baby.
**Cherry**
Please! Oh please! What's wrong with me? Look! Look! Look at me! My body!
> *She rips off her negligee and kneels naked in front of* GEEZ.

I'm young! I'm ravishing! Look at my fine oval milk white breasts. The erect nipples trembling with ecstatic antici-pation of the savage touch of your pounding thumbs!
**Geez**
Pretty nice.
**Cherry**
Who could ask for more? Take me with you! Take me! Take me!
**Geez**
There's nowhere to go. This is it. Dead end city.
**Cherry**
There must be a way out. The helicopter! The helicopter!
> *She rushes to* D.T. *and searches through his pockets for the keys as* D.T. *holds his wound and moans.*

Where are the keys? The keys! We can fly away from here!

Just the two of us! We can go to Tangiers or Nice or Rome or somewhere. Where are the keys? The keys!

**D.T.**

No! Stay away! I'm dying!

**Geez**

I don't know the first thing about putting that crate in the air.

**Cherry**

He does.

**Geez**

He's dying.

**Cherry**

Get up! D.T., get up! You're going to fly us out of here!

**D.T.**

I've been shot.

**Geez**

Leave him alone.

**Cherry**

Well, what about me? You don't care if you die. He *wants* to die. Wong doesn't even know what's going on. But what about me?

**Geez**

What about you?

**Cherry**

I want to live. They won't kill me anyway. They want you. They're only after you.

**Geez**

That's right. The safest place is under the bed.

> CHERRY *pauses a moment, thinking. Then she scrambles under the bed and disappears. GEEZ sits on the bed with his rifle. D.T. moans. WONG dances as GEEZ watches him. Things get quieter. The dance gets slower and slower, then WONG stops. He holds very still and slowly takes off his mask. He looks at GEEZ.*

**Cherry**

What's going on out there?

> GEEZ *and* WONG *stare into each other's eyes. GEEZ doesn't speak. Then WONG walks to the window and looks out. He*

> *climbs up on the windowsill and jumps out. Silence.* GEEZ
> *just sits on the bed.*

What's happening?

**Geez**

Gone.

**Cherry**

What?

**Geez**

They're gone.

**Cherry**

Who? The police?

**Geez**

They'll be back.

**Cherry**

Is something wrong? Where's Wong? What's happened to
Wong?

**Geez**

He jumped out the window.

**Cherry**

He did not. Where is he?

**Geez**

Very peaceful eyes. Chinese.

**Cherry**

Why is everything so quiet?

**D.T.**

I could have had a life of my own. I had talent once. Am-
bition.

**Geez**

Just sit it out. Like hunting deer. Waiting and waiting and
being very still. Being part of the breeze. Acting like a leaf.

**Cherry**

Maybe they left.

**D.T.**

You get caught up for no reason. I just found myself in a
corporation. Incorporated. Nice operation.

**Geez**

A deer lives in fear. Right up to the end. Twitching ears.

Big wet nose. Smelling, sniffing. Ducks his head down long enough for a sip of crystal clear water. Ears twitch and the head bobs back up with water drops dripping off her lips. Big loving eyes. You can't look at the eyes or they'll break your heart.

**Cherry**

Maybe I should come out now. Do you think it's O.K.?

**Geez**

Then one blast that shatters the whole forest. Everything bolts and screams. The doe twists in a circle, the rear end sinking to the ground, the front hooves thrashing, the head points straight at the sky.

**D.T.**

I knew what I was geting myself into. I was aware.

**Geez**

You ever seen a deer skinned?

**Cherry**

No. And I don't give a damn. Just tell me if it's all right to come out.

**Geez**

It hangs by its hind legs on two big hooks with its head pointing down. You use a big sharp knife and slice the skin away from the fetlocks. There's a milky white membrane that holds the outside skin to the inside skin. You slice the membrane with downward strokes and pull the skin slowly away from the body. There's no blood. Very neat. By the time you're through there's a naked white carcass hanging upside down with all its skin hung around its head. Then you cut the head off and you've got a head with all the hide attached. Very neat.

**Cherry**

What's going on anyway?

**Geez**

The war's over.

**D.T.**

I could have fought. It wasn't an act of cowardice. I was born with a bad back. They wouldn't accept me.

*GEEZ'S VOICE comes over the P.A. He follows the directions of the voice. D.T. lies on the floor gasping for breath and dying.*

**Geez's Voice**
Geez rose from the spot, his rifle slung over his shoulder.
*He stands with his back to audience and slings his rifle on his shoulder.*
He gazed across the ravaged rubble of the city. His mind went back to Tucson and Albuquerque where it all began. Somehow he'd reached the end of the road. Nothing lay ahead and nothing behind. His heart sank. The blazing hot ball of a sun baked his shoulders and twisted his brain. He had to take a step. He had to make a move somehow. If things could only be simple and easy again.
*The lights begin to fade as GEEZ just stands and D.T. dies.*
But now the war was over. Peace was the hard part. He was a man of the gun. It was all he knew. In the distance the lonely whistle of the Rock Island Line teased at his ears. How many boxcars? How many years had it been since he'd last seen the shaggy prairies of his youth? Cheyenne, Wyoming. Baton Rouge, Tucumcari, Boise. The places ran across his mind like a speeded-up movie. Now, everywhere the stench of the dead and the dying. Smoke curled through the lobby of a gutted-out movie house. How he yearned for a movie. Any movie. Just to sit and watch and drink Pepsi Cola and eat popcorn and chew Abazabas and spit on the floor and smoke Camels. But all that was gone. All those wild crazy days. Now it was him. Just him alone. No more crowds to get lost in. He moved down the street slowly, kicking empty raisin boxes and blackened bottles. Somewhere in his mind a band was playing. Chuck Berry, Elvis Presley, Little Richard, Rolling Stones, Fats Domino music. All combined. All the sounds of the fifties and sixties combined in one band and all making sense. All making music. Then it seemed it came from the street itself. From out of the smoke and rubble. From out of the gutted tenements and ramshackle shacks. He followed the music like a dog scenting deer. It

seemed to draw him up off his feet. He began to feel like a man again. He turned through twisted mounds of metal and steel following the sound until he came to a bar with the windows blown out and over the door hung a sign that read "Bird Dog Man." He walked inside, kicking aside a hubcap from a '49 Pontiac. There in the dingy back room, high up on the bandstand the band was playing "Satisfaction." They were pounding it out like they'd been doing it for a million years. He crept a little closer, afraid to disturb their deep concentration. Suddenly his eyes caught sight of a bright orange guitar all plugged in and ready to go. Nobody was using it. If he only knew how. If someone had only showed him how when he was young and eager to learn. He didn't care. He was going to play it anyway. He was going to sit down and play the damn thing. He set down his rifle carefully in a corner and walked over to the guitar. He picked it up and something happened to his hands. Gold light shot out from his hands and they began to move over the guitar in patterns and rhythms he'd never seen before. He was playing! He was playing lead for the greatest band in the world. He looked up and all the musicians were smiling from ear to ear. It was as though they knew he was coming. The music filled him up and poured out over the dusty tables and chairs. He was alive again. The war was over and he was alive!

## THE END

# 4-H Club

(1964)

# Scene:

An empty stage except for a small kitchén extreme upstage left. Three flats compose the walls of the kitchen with a swinging door in the upstage wall. On the floor downstage left of the kitchen is a hot plate with a coffee pot on it. The floor of the kitchen is littered with paper, cans and various trash. There is a garbage can in the upstage right corner. The walls are very dirty. The lighting should be equal for the whole stage with no attempt to focus light on the kitchen. The lights come up slowly. JOHN is downstage facing the audience kneeling beside the hot plate. He is stirring something in the pot with a spoon. BOB stands in the middle of the kitchen jumping up and down and laughing wildly. JOE stands upstage beside the door with a broom. He is hitting the door with the broom and laughing with BOB. They are all dressed in torn, grimy clothes. BOB and JOE laugh hysterically and fall to their knees. They fall on the floor and roll around stomping their feet. They stop laughing. A pause. JOHN hits the spoon on the pot several times.

**John**

You can't call it coffee anymore. Brown powder for coffee, white powder for cream, saccharine for sugar. Water's the only thing that stays the same. Put it all together and it comes out coffee.

**Bob**

Put it all together.

**John**

I am.

**Joe**

Three.

**John**

Three colored waters.

> *He pours water out of the pot into three coffee cups; he hands a cup to BOB, and a cup to JOE, then sits on the floor with the last cup. BOB and JOE sit; a pause as they all sit and drink from the cups. BOB slurps, a pause, JOE slurps loudly, JOHN slurps even louder. They all stand suddenly and smash the cups on the floor. BOB and JOHN start kicking the pieces back and forth across the kitchen.*

**Joe**

Hey! Hey! Cut it out! Stop!

> *He grabs the broom and tries to sweep up the pieces as JOHN and BOB continue kicking them.*

Cut it out! Stop it! We got to keep this place neat! Cut it out! Stop!

> *BOB and JOHN stop and watch JOE as he sweeps the pieces into a pile.*

**John**

That's very nice, Joe.

**Joe**

Thanks.

**John**

It's neat the way you're sweeping that all up nice and neat.

**Joe**

Thanks.

**John**
Could I do it, Joe?
**Joe**
Nope.
**John**
Come on.
**Joe**
Nope.

> *A pause as JOE continues sweeping. He gets the pieces into
> a pile, then looks at JOHN and BOB. BOB and JOHN kick
> the pieces all over the floor, then run out the door laughing.
> JOE looks after them, then starts sweeping again.*

I don't care myself. I mean it doesn't matter to me
about the neatness part of it. I was thinking in terms
of someday having bare feet and walking in here and
getting cut.

> *He continues sweeping.*

That's all. I'm leaving the country anyway, so it doesn't
matter.

> *He stops and yells at the door.*

It don't make no difference! Hear me?

> *He starts sweeping again.*

Not just glass, either. There's bottle caps and tin can
edges and razor blades too. All the stuff that cuts is
bad for bare feet. That's all I was thinking of as far as
sweeping goes. As far as clean goes, if I was thinking
of clean we could get a fire hose in here and blast the
walls and the floors and the stove. Just a great huge
blast of hot water. That would do it.

> *He goes to the garbage can and drags it over to the pile of
> glass. He puts the pile into the can as he continues talking.*

You'd need permission, I guess. How much would it
cost to hire a fireman for one day to blast this place?
I don't think he'd do it. It would knock down the walls,
anyway. It would probably wash the stove out into the
audience. It'd take a week to dry anyway. There'd be
puddles of water all over the floor.

> *He drags the garbage can back into the corner, then
> crosses down to the hot plate.*

No good. Leave it as it is for the time being. I'm going anyway.

*He looks into the coffee pot.*

Coffee.

*JOHN enters through the door eating an apple. He stands upstage of the kitchen watching JOE and eating the apple with loud crunches.*

Water and powder. That's kind of bad when you think about it. If a fire starts, all they do is knock down the walls with blasts of water. They have to build all over again anyway.

**John**

*Still upstage.*

It puts the fire out, though.

**Joe**

*Without turning around.*

Yeah, but the walls are all broken down. Hunks of wet wood and pieces of cement all broken to pieces. Do they put floods out with fire? Nope. It works the other way around.

**John**

It's chemical. Oxygen. Water cuts off oxygen. Simple.

**Joe**

Then all the firemen stand around in puddles of water and grin. The fire's been stopped and all the people stand there in puddles of water looking at this mound of rubbish with smoke rising off it. Then the firemen grin some more and coil up the hoses and put them back on the trucks and ride off into the night grinning and waving. And all the people stand there looking at this mound of rubbish.

*He turns around suddenly and looks at JOHN.*

**John**

What?

**Joe**

An apple!

**John**

Yeah.

**Joe**
Where'd you get it?
**John**
It's mine.
**Joe**
Where'd you get it?
**John**
None of your business.
> JOE *approaches* JOHN *slowly;* JOHN *backs up.*

**Joe**
Come on, John. That's a brand new red apple.
**John**
So what?
**Joe**
So it crunches.
**John**
Crunches?
**Joe**
Crunches. It sounds good.
> JOE *approaches* JOHN *slowly.* JOHN *backs up in a circle around the kitchen.*

**John**
It is good. It's a "Washington Delicious."
**Joe**
It looks delicious, John.
**John**
Get back.
**Joe**
I've eaten green apples before, but never a bright red one.
**John**
Green ones are for cooking.
**Joe**
Red and crunchy.
**John**
Yeah. Get back!

**Joe**
A "Washington Delicious."
**John**
Look, stay away from my apple, Joe.
**Joe**
Apple juice! We could make a lot of apple juice.
**John**
I'm eating it!
> *He takes big bites out of the apple as JOE continues backing him up.*

**Joe**
Take it easy! You're eating it all up.
**John**
It's mine, stupid! Of course I'm eating it.
**Joe**
What about the juice?
**John**
That was your idea. Get back.
**Joe**
We could salt it.
**John**
No salt!
**Joe**
We could cut it into little slices and put salt on it. Come on, John. Diced apple is what they call it.
> *They go faster in a circle, JOHN backing up and eating the apple as JOE follows.*

We'd leave the skin on it for more protein. We could eat the seeds and boil the core. Apple core soup we could have. We'd put salt in that too. Salt and pepper. Maybe some sugar and salt and pepper. It'd last for days, John. A whole week of diced apple soup and sugar. Stewing. That's a whole stewing apple you have in your hand. A bright red "Washington Delicious" stewing apple for us to eat!
> *JOHN runs out the door laughing. JOE yells at the door, standing in the middle of the kitchen.*

Fuck your apple, John! Apples grow on trees! Green

and red ones, John! As many as you can carry in your pockets and stuffed inside your shirt! One apple is nothing compared to what I've seen! And I've seen plenty, John! Don't forget that! I'll bring some when I get back! I'll bring all the apples I can get my hands on! A ton! There's apples all over, you know. Not just Washington!

*He starts talking to himself. He walks aimlessly around the kitchen kicking pieces of trash on the floor.*

"Washington Delicious" is a brand name. It doesn't fool anybody. They grow all over the place. It's a stupid thing to name apples anyway. "Florida Oranges." There's another one. "Maine Cherries!" "Wisconsin Cheese!" "Minnesota Watercress!" "Arizona Spinach!"

*He starts kicking the trash violently and yelling.*

"New Jersey Cottage Cheese!" "Nebraska Mayonnaise!" "Oklahoma Malted Milk!" "California Scrambled Eggs!" "Viet Nam Corn on the Cob!" "Mexico Peanut Butter!" "Alaska Turnips!"

*He stops, crosses downstage and looks into the coffee pot. A pause.*

Hey, John! Hey, John and Bob! Do you want some coffee? That water's boiling. It's all hot and ready. Hot boiling coffee for you people if you want it!

*He turns to the door.*

Hey! The coffee's ready! You guys bring the apples in here and I'll give you some coffee. There's enough for three! I know you guys have apples! I know you have all the apples you need and I have the coffee!

*BOB enters through the door eating an apple. He stands upstage facing JOE.*

Hi, Bob.

**Bob**

Hi.

*He stares at JOE and takes large bites out of the apple.*

**Joe**

Do you want some coffee?

**Bob**

We broke the cups.

**Joe**
Yeah, I know.
**Bob**
We couldn't drink coffee out of the pot.
**Joe**
I guess not.
**Bob**
How would we drink it?
**Joe**
Well, I don't know.
**Bob**
We don't have any more cups around.
**Joe**
I guess not.
**Bob**
The water's ready, huh?
**Joe**
Yeah, it's all ready.
**Bob**
Gee, I could really go for some coffee.
**Joe**
Me too.

> *They start walking in a circle slowly as they talk to each other,* JOE *following* BOB.

**Bob**
It's too bad we broke all the cups.
**Joe**
Yeah.
**Bob**
We could be having coffee right now if it wasn't for that.
**Joe**
With cream and sugar.
**Bob**
However you take it.
**Joe**
We could be sitting around on the floor talking and drinking.

**Bob**
Yeah. It would have been nice.
**Joe**
It's too bad.
**Bob**
Maybe we'll do it sometime.
**Joe**
Sure.
**Bob**
We'll get some more cups and sit around drinking.
*They both start laughing as they circle the kitchen.*
**Joe**
We'll even clean the floor so we can sit down.
**Bob**
We'll get all this junk out of here.
**Joe**
We'll clear it all away. We'll put it in the can and throw it in the street.
**Bob**
Throw it out the window.
**Joe**
We'll hit somebody in the head.
**Bob**
It'll smash somebody in the head.
**Joe**
That's a heavy can.
**Bob**
It'd really smash, wouldn't it?
*They laugh harder.*
**Joe**
It'd break to pieces.
**Bob**
We'd kill a lot of people with that can.
**Joe**
Little kids and old ladies. Some old lady buying pota-toes for her invalid husband.
**Bob**
Right!

**Joe**
She's down there limping along with a bag full of potatoes, and this garbage can smashes her in the head.
**Bob**
Potatoes all over the street!
**Joe**
She wouldn't even know what hit her!
**Bob**
Then after that there's a whole crowd of people. They come running from all over. The whole street is running toward this old lady with her head smashed in.
**Joe**
They're yelling and screaming and trying to get a look.
**Bob**
There's more and more people!
**Joe**
All over!
**Bob**
Then do you know what we do?
**Joe**
What?
**Bob**
We're looking out the window, see.
**Joe**
Yeah?
**Bob**
And we start throwing apples!
**Joe**
Right! Right!
> BOB *tosses the apple to* JOE. *They throw it back and forth, laughing harder and still going in a circle.*

**Bob**
We could hide behind the window so they wouldn't know where they were coming from.
**Joe**
Apples out of the sky!

**Bob**
Right! All these apples sailing through the air and crashing their skulls!

**Joe**
More and more people come. They think it's a riot or something.

**Bob**
They call the cops!

**Joe**
There's sirens all over!

**Bob**
Everybody's head is bloody from the apples!

**Joe**
They're lying in the street moaning and groaning.

**Bob**
The cops can't figure it out!

**Joe**
The cops get hit. There's dead cops lying on the sidewalk with bloody heads.

**Bob**
Apples!

**Joe**
They call the National Guard!

**Bob**
They bring tanks! A whole string of armored cars and tanks charging up the street.

**Joe**
Apples from the sky!

**Bob**
They shoot at the sky!

**Joe**
*Get back in your houses, ladies and gentlemen! There's apples falling out here!*

**Bob**
*This is an emergency, people!*

**Joe**
*We're going to shoot the sky and we don't want any-
one to get hurt!*

**Bob**
*Stay inside your houses! We shall open fire in exactly
ten seconds!*
> BOB *catches the apple and holds it. They both start making
> gun sounds and firing at the sky. They stop going in a circle.*

**Joe**
*Pow! Blam!*

**Bob**
We're getting them, ladies and gentlemen! Just stay
inside! There's a lot of apples left!

**Joe**
Blam! Blam! Blam! I think we're winning!

**Bob**
Pow! Blam! I think we've done it!
> *To the audience.*

Ladies and gentlemen, this is the end of the apples.
> JOHN *enters through the door eating an apple.* BOB *and* JOE
> *sit on the floor.* JOHN *stares at them.*

**John**
Is there any coffee?

**Bob**
Nope.

**Joe**
There's coffee but no cups.

**John**
That's too bad.
> *He goes out the door.*

**Bob**
> *Still sitting.*

We should clean up, you know.

**Joe**
Yeah.

**Bob**
Just a little sweeping and some elbow grease.

**Joe**
I don't mind sweeping.
**Bob**
Me neither.
**Joe**
I used to sweep driveways a lot.
**Bob**
Really?
**Joe**
Yeah. Leaves. The driveways would get covered with leaves and dirt so I'd sweep them for a quarter.
**Bob**
A quarter each?
**Joe**
Yeah. They were long driveways though, so it wasn't as easy as it sounds.
**Bob**
I guess not.
**Joe**
Six in the morning I'd start.
**Bob**
How come so early?
**Joe**
I don't know. I just wanted to get up. I'd do the whole block before eight o'clock.
**Bob**
That's pretty fast.
**Joe**
Sometimes I'd use a hose. Just spray the leaves down the driveway and into the street.
**Bob**
That was probably faster.
**Joe**
Yeah. They paid by the job, not by the hour, so it didn't matter.

    JOHN *enters through the door again and stands watching*

*JOE and* BOB *as they continue to talk.* JOHN *and* BOB *eat their apples slowly.*

**Bob**

I just cut lawns.

**Joe**

I did some of that too. Trouble was there was this older guy who sort of had a monopoly on all the lawns.

**Bob**

Oh yeah?

**Joe**

Yeah. He was old enough to drive, see, and he had a car, a station wagon. He had all kinds of power tools that he used. Power mowers and edgers and hedge clippers. Things like that. And he was a kissy. I mean he'd smile at all the old ladies that owned all the lawns and he'd bring their milk in for them in the mornings and their newspapers. He was like a trained dog, sort of. He even went on errands because some of them couldn't walk. He'd buy them orange juice and cod liver oil and calcium tablets, all that junk. Then he moved in on them. He started vacuuming their rugs and polishing their silver and washing their dishes. They really loved this guy. He was like their son or something.

**John**

Sounds like a fairy.

**Joe**

After a while he bought a new car—a truck, rather. A bright red pickup truck, and he painted white letters on the side of it that said "Mike's Gardening Service." He wasn't even out of high school and he owned a whole business. He cut every old lady's lawn in the whole town. He even had a telephone number in case of emergency.

**Bob**

Like a doctor.

**Joe**

Right. They'd call him in the middle of the night sometimes.

**Bob**

How come?

**Joe**

I don't know. But he was making more and more money. Then more old ladies started moving into the town. One after the other. They heard about this guy, see, and they came from all over. They all bought a little white house with a green lawn and a driveway. He was so busy he had to hire some help. He had a whole crew of special gardeners after a while. I was his special driveway sweeper. He had one man for each job and he just came around to check on us. He started wearing a suit and he'd drive up in his truck just to see how we were doing.

> JOHN *crosses downstage and looks into the coffee pot as* JOE *continues.*

He quit school after a while because the business got so big. And the town was growing. A whole town of old ladies with green lawns and white houses. He'd visit them and have tea and cake and talk about their lawns and their driveways. The mayor even gave him a prize for improving the community. Then he started giving speeches at luncheons and benefits. They paid him lots of money to talk in front of all these groups. He'd talk about horticulture and fertilizer and ground improvement plans. Then he started giving talks on zoning and housing facilities. He drew up a whole plan for a children's recreation area. All these old ladies were going to let him build a children's recreation area and pay him to boot. He got bigger and bigger and richer and richer until one day he left the town. He just drove off in a Rolls Royce or something and all those old ladies died. One at a time.

**Bob**

What do you mean?

**Joe**

They just died. Nobody new came to the town after that. The houses got all dirty and the lawns grew out into the driveways and the leaves covered all the sidewalks.

**Bob**

They died?

**Joe**

That's what they said.

> JOHN *kneels facing the audience and stares at the audience as* JOE *continues.*

**Bob**

Who?

**Joe**

All the guys. We'd go into the town sometimes on week-ends. We had to get a bunch of guys together because we were all scared. We hiked into the town and then waited till it got dark. Those were the rules. It had to be dark. Then one of us would go at a time. Each one of us walked from one end of the town to the other. The thing was, we had to keep our eyes closed. We couldn't look. We could just feel the sidewalk with our feet. That's all we had to go on. If we touched the grass we knew we were getting lost. This one guy, Ernie, he got lost once and wandered right into one of the houses. He told us later that he was in this tiny living room with a fireplace. There were all these books lying around on the floor and big tall lamps with yellow lampshades and pictures of swallows and dogs hung on the walls. There was a little round table with a checkerboard and a chess set. Then he told us that he went through this doorway with beaded curtains hanging in it. He walked down this hallway and he could smell all the wallpaper. Then he walked into a huge bathroom that was painted blue and there was this old lady lying on her stomach with a spoon in her hand.

> JOHN *slams the coffee pot down on the hot plate.*
> BOB *and* JOE *stand suddenly.*

**John**

The water's cold!

> *He stands still facing the audience.*

**Joe**
It was just boiling.
**John**
Now it's cold.
**Bob**
It was boiling before, John. We were going to have some coffee.
**John**
Yeah. Well, cold coffee doesn't exactly turn me on. I thought you were leaving, Joe.
**Joe**
I am.
**John**
When?
**Joe**
When I can.
**John**
When can you, Joe?
**Joe**
I'm not sure.
**John**
Well, before you were yelling about it, and now you're not sure. You were yelling, "It doesn't matter because I'm leaving the country!"
**Joe**
I know.
**John**
Then you started yelling about apples or something.
**Bob**
We both were.
**John**
I remember.
**Bob**
We were both doing that.
**John**
I remember! I remember! Now the water's cold and there aren't any cups!

**Joe**
We broke them.
**Bob**
You broke one of them, John. Remember?
**John**
I remember that! Seems like we could make some soup or something.
**Joe**
Sure.
**John**
Sure! And sweep! Clean up the kitchen, Goddamnit! We can't eat apples in a dirty kitchen!
**Bob**
It's all right, John.
**John**
*He turns upstage and paces back and forth kicking the debris on the floor.*
It's all right, John! It's all right! Rats don't eat much. They don't eat apples. Rats eat cheese. Rats and mice and everything nice.
**Joe**
There's no mice, John.
**John**
There's no mice, John! The mice ran away. They went away for food. They left the country! A whole troop of mice marched out the door and said, "Fuck it! We're going to go out! We're going to hunt some food on our own! We're going to get fat and lie around burping all day!"
**Bob**
We'll clean it up.
**John**
Clean it up! Clean it up! Forget it! The apples are running out and the mice don't care anyway so just forget it!
*He goes out through the door.*

**Bob**
> *Yelling at the door.*

John! There aren't any mice around here! John!

**Joe**
> *Yelling at the door.*

John! The mice are all gone! There's none left!

**John**
> *Offstage.*

There's some around. I've seen them.

**Bob**

Where?

**John**

Inside the walls. In the garbage can. All over!

**Bob**

They're all gone, John!

**John**

You just haven't looked!

**Bob**

I'll look.
> *He looks in the garbage can and then under the hot plate.*

**John**

They're hard to see. They're grayish and small so they blend right into the floor. You probably can't find them.

**Joe**

There's none here, John!

**John**

They're there if you look.

**Bob**

I don't see them, John.

**John**

They're there!
> JOE *looks in the garbage can, then searches around the floor.*
> BOB *does the same.*

**Bob**

They couldn't just hide, John. It's impossible.

**Joe**

We'd hear them wriggling around.

**John**
> *Still off.*

They're very quiet.

**Bob**

They're just small little animals. They wouldn't have a chance.

**Joe**

We'd kill them!

**John**

They bite. They have sharp little razor teeth and they cut.
> BOB *and* JOE *start kicking the trash and looking for the mice.*

**Joe**

They're all skinny and weak, John. They don't stand a chance.

**Bob**

One smash of the foot and it'd be all over.

**John**

They're tough.

**Joe**

They're too weak, John.

**Bob**

They're flimsy little animals. They run.

**John**

They don't scare easy.

**Bob**

They're all gone, John.

**Joe**

You just stomp them on the head, John.
> *They kick the trash and look on the floor.*

**Bob**

You break their necks.

**Joe**

We'd hear them if they were in here. We'd hear them moving around.

**Bob**
There's none left, John.
**John**
They're there.
**Joe**
All you do is squash them!
**Bob**
> *Stomping his foot on the floor.*
*Smash!*
**Joe**
*Squash!*
**Bob**
*Smash!*
> BOB *and* JOE *stomp their feet loudly on the floor, yelling the lines.*
**Joe**
Come out, mice! *Smash!*
**Bob**
Crush the mice! *Crunch! Crunch!*
**Joe**
Little tiny mouse bones! *Smash!*
**John**
You'll never find them! They hide!
**Bob**
*Crunch! Smash!*
**Joe**
Little gray-headed mice!
**John**
They're in the walls!
**Bob**
We'll smash your heads!
**Joe**
Come out, mice! *Smash!*
**Bob**
Break your backs!
**Joe**
*Smash! Crunch!*

**Bob**

Come out! Come out!

**Joe**

Little gray mothers! We'll squash your heads to pieces!
> *He goes to the garbage can and dumps it out on the floor.
> BOB and JOE kick the garbage all over, yelling and scream-
> ing. They jump up and down wildly.*

**Bob**

You don't stand a chance!

**Joe**

We're big! *Squash! Crunch!*

**Bob**

Come out, mice! You're dead!

**Joe**

We'll make some soup!

**Bob**

You're dead, mice!
> *BOB picks up the broom and hits it against the door.*

**Joe**

It's all over, mice! Your time is up!

**Bob**

*Smash!* It's all over! Come out!

**Joe**

We have big feet, mice! Big strong feet with shoes!

**Bob**

We'll bust your heads!

**Joe**

Kill the mice!

**Bob**

*Come out! Come out!*
> *The lights black out in the kitchen; the rest of the stage re-
> mains in light. JOHN walks slowly into the bare stage area
> from behind the kitchen. He is eating an apple and carries
> several apples inside his shirt. He crosses downstage right
> and stands looking at the kitchen while he eats the apple.
> BOB and JOE continue yelling inside the kitchen.*

**Joe**

You don't have a chance!

**Bob**
You'll die if you show your face!
**Joe**
Come on, chickens! We see you!
**Bob**
Come out of there!
**Joe**
We can see your eyes! We know you're there!
**Bob**
Show yourself!
**Joe**
Smashed to death by a foot!
**Bob**
*Crash! Crunch! Die!*
**Joe**
*Kill! Smash!* Come out of there!
**Bob**
Give it up, mouse!
**Joe**
Give it up! Come on out!
**Bob**
You're dead!
**Joe**
We see you! We know you guys!
**Bob**
We can see you!
**Joe**
We know you're there! Come out!
**Bob**
You guys have had it!
**Joe**
Come on out!
> *They stop banging their feet.*
**Bob**
All right, you guys, come on. We know you're in there!
**Joe**
You can come out now.

**Bob**
It's all over, you guys.
**Joe**
You can come out now.
**Bob**
You're not fooling anyone.
**Joe**
Mouse! Come out. We can see you in there!
**Bob**
Come out of there before we get you.
**Joe**
We could tear this place apart with our bare hands. You know that, don't you?
**Bob**
We're bigger than you—let's face it.
**Joe**
Mice?
**Bob**
We have all the strength. You're too little.
**Joe**
We'll wait for you. We'll wait here all night until you decide.
**Bob**
You'll have to come out sooner or later.
**Joe**
You're going to be sorry.

> BOB *and* JOE *sit on either side of the kitchen and light ciga-rettes.* JOHN *continues to crunch loudly on the apple.*

**Bob**
John? We're going to wait for them.
**John**
Good.

> *He leans against the proscenium down right.*

**Bob**
It won't take long. If we're quiet they'll think we left.
**John**
O.K.

**Bob**
We could tear the place apart, but it's easier to wait.

**John**
Sure.

**Bob**
So don't come in for a while.

**John**
I won't.

**Bob**
Good.

**Joe**
There's probably just a couple of them anyway, John. It won't take long to do.

**John**
Good.

**Joe**
They might have a family, though, so it may take longer. I mean a whole bunch of babies. We'll just step on them and sweep them up later.

**Bob**
There'll be a little blood, though. We may have to boil some water and scrub the place down. The walls and the floor.

**Joe**
Yeah. There'll be some blood on the walls, John. They spurt when you step on them. Especially the babies.

**Bob**
The babies haven't grown any fur yet, so they're more fragile. Their skin is very thin and they just pop open.

**Joe**
They look like little embryos. They can't see because their eyes haven't opened yet. They're blind, so it'll be easier to get them.

**John**
Don't you think you should be quieter?

**Joe**
> *Whispering.*

You're right, John. We have to be quiet, Bob.

**Bob**
> *Whispering.*

Sit very still.

**John**

It may take a while, you know.

**Joe**
> *Whispering.*

It's all right. We'll wait.

**John**

They can hear you breathing. It's very hard to trick a mouse. I've tried everything from baseball bats to machetes. I even tried throwing hatchets, but it was no good.

**Joe**
> *Whispering.*

He's right. My uncle even used a shotgun and that didn't work.

**John**

I used pistols and swords and everything, and they kept coming back. I sat very still until they showed their heads. Then I'd fire. I emptied a whole chamber into this one mouse and he just limped away.

**Bob**
> *Whispering.*

Did he die?

**John**

Nope. He just kept coming back. I kept shooting him and he kept coming back. Then he had lots of babies that followed him around. There was blood all over the house, but none of them died.

**Joe**
> *Whispering.*

Did they bite?

**John**
I never let them get that close. I never gave them a chance.

*A pause as JOHN crunches loudly on the apple.*

**Bob**
    *Whispering.*
Sure wish we had some coffee.

**Joe**
Yeah.

**Bob**
    *Whispering.*
I saw a man hit a mouse with a wrench one time and the mouse just ran away.

**Joe**
    *Whispering.*
Maybe it was a rat. Rats are bigger.

**Bob**
It might have been a rat. It had a long tail. It didn't hurt him at all, though. It just made a big cracking sound. He hit him right in the head too.

**John**
Rats are different. More ferocious. They can actually charge you if they get into a corner.

**Bob**
    *Whispering.*
It had big huge fangs on each side of its mouth. There was all this green pussy stuff hanging off them.

**John**
They carry tetanus and different bacteria. Some Indian tribe uses rat pus for poison arrows. It kills the victim instantly.

**Joe**
    *Whispering.*
They carry that junk on their tails too. And their feet. All you have to do is brush up against them and you die.

**John**
Rats usually go around in large groups. Ten at a time.

They're like coyotes in that respect. Constantly ravenous. They can never get enough to eat.

*He takes another apple out of his shirt and tosses it up in the air and then catches it. He continues to do this as he talks.*

Baboons too. There's one kind of baboon called a mandrill that is known as the fiercest animal in the world. I think it's a toss-up really between the mandrill and the wolverine. Wolverines run in packs too. Twenty or thirty at once.

**Bob**

*Whispering.*

They close their eyes in the dark when they know they're being watched. That way you can't see them. You can't see their eyes.

**John**

I'll send you some postcards when I get there. They have big color postcards of the mandrills. They're hard to find because photographers are afraid to go into that area. Only a few have survived.

**Joe**

*Whispering.*

We couldn't tell if they were here or not, Bob. They may be walking around in here right now. I mean if they close their eyes like you said.

**Bob**

They do.

**Joe**

Maybe we should make some noise to scare them off.

**Bob**

No.

**John**

The country around there is really beautiful. Completely wild. There's little patches of green woods and tiny lakes where the mandrills go to drink water. There's a few small villages inhabited by fishermen and hunters.

**Joe**

We should make some noise, Bob.

**Bob**
No. Sit still.

**John**
The plane goes right over the area and you can look out the window and see these long beaches and fishing boats all lined up.

**Bob**
*Whispering.*
Sit very still.

**John**
There's a guide on the plane who tells you all you need to know about mandrills.

**Bob**
Very quiet. They'll never see us.

**John**
He says they have red and blue faces and no hair on their rumps. They're about twice as big as a chimpanzee and have brownish red hair.

**Joe**
Can you see them?

**Bob**
Shhh!

**John**
They're mainly carnivorous but will occasionally eat succulent plants that grow near the lake. Their incisors are surprisingly dog-like and they are known to pick their teeth with bones.

**Joe**
*Whispering.*
We should make some noise.

**Bob**
*Whispering.*
Sit still.

**John**
The guide shows the specific areas where the mandrills live and warns the passengers to keep clear of them. He says they are extremely temperamental and will

charge a human without any provocation. He says they scream in high staccato voices and run on all fours. They charge in groups of four and tear mercilessly at the victim's throat. They cut the jugular vein and then rip the head off. They eat the brain first, then devour the body. They tear off the arms and legs and carry them back to their mates.

**Joe**

*Yelling.*

We have to make some noise!

**Bob**

*Yelling.*

No!

*JOE goes to the coffee pot and starts banging it on the hot plate. BOB wrestles with him in the dark.*

**Joe**

We'll scare them away, Bob!

**Bob**

No noise! Stop!

*They continue wrestling as JOHN keeps talking.*

**John**

It's always good weather for some reason. I mean every time I've gone there the sun has always been out and the air has been clear. The water is so blue you can see all the way to the bottom. Clear as a bell.

**Bob**

Cut it out, Joe!

*JOE keeps banging the pot on the hot plate in a steady rhythm.*

**Joe**

Noise! We have to make some noise!

**Bob**

Stop it! No noise!

**Joe**

Loud! Loud! Loud!

**John**

Then you land and go to the hotel. The air smells so good you can taste it. They have breakfast all ready for you. It's sitting there on this glass table in front of a huge picture window. You just sit there and eat and look out over the ocean.

> JOE *continues banging the coffee pot in a steady rhythm as the lights dim down slowly.*

**Bob**
No noise, Joe! Stop! No noise!

**Joe**
Louder! Get away! Loud! Loud!

**John**
I'll send you some postcards. I'll buy a dozen or so and send one a week. It's a great place. I'm going to do some swimming too. Floating on my back. You just float and stare at the sky. You just float and stare at the sky. You just float and stare at the sky. You just float and stare at the sky.

> *The lights dim out as* JOE *continues banging the coffee pot in a steady beat.*

## THE END